8TH JULY 11
DARREY

28TH JULY 11
DARREM

BW

West Sussex County Council Library

Please return/renew this item by the last
date shown. Books may also be renewed
by phone 01243 642110 or the Internet.

ᴠ.westsussex.gov.uk

 west
sussex
county
council

About the authors

Dutch-born **Remmert Wielinga** is a former professional cyclist who has competed in numerous international races since he started cycling at the age of 12, including the Tour de France. In 1999 he won the Dutch national championships time trial. The following year he joined the Rabobank Continental Team and repeated his victory in the national championships. In 2001 Remmert signed his first professional contract with the Italian cycling team De Nardi-Pasta Montegrappa where learned the revolutionary methods on effective physical training and conditioning. During his professional career he raced for world-famous teams including Rabobank, Quick-Step and Saunier Duval, where he trained and competed side-by-side with world-renowned cyclists. In 2003 Remmert won two races in Spain and in 2006 finished first in the GP Chiasso in Switzerland after an impressive breakaway of 150 kilometres (93 miles). Remmert is based in Monaco where he runs his company, Cycling Promotions (www.cyclingpromotions.mc) that provides specialized personal coaching services

Paul Cowcher has been working in the health and fitness industry since 2001 after a career as a professional dancer (musicals in London's West End and touring). When his dancing career was over he recognized there were many similarities between dancing and sports and science. He has trained as an advanced instructor (CYQ), Pilates mat work (More Fitness) and has over 10 other teaching qualifications in fitness and dance (ISTD.) He now works as a personal trainer.

Tommaso Bernabei is a television and non-fiction writer who graduated from the Metropolitan University of London. His experience in television led him to collaborate with Italian food shows, introducing him into the world of sport nutrition. He is currently the diet planner for an Italian swimming club and writing a book of sport nutrition recipes.

Thanks to Kees Wielinga.

Photo Credits

iStockphoto.com and jacket, p18 Fabian-serwis – www.wikimedia.org. p18 Qw345 – www.wikimedia.org. p18, p57 Paul Chessare – http://www.generalatomic.us, www.sxc.hu. p22, p156 David Ritter – www.sxc.hu. p22 Cienpies Design – http://www.cienpies.net, www.sxc.hu. p22 Ramasamy Chidambaram – www.studiosrishti.com, www.sxc.hu. p43 TJBlackwell – www.wikimedia.org. p47 Horemu – www.wikimedia.org. p53 Becky Brandt – http://brandt-photography.com, www.sxc.hu. p59 and p60 Press Association Images. p88 John Evans – www.thetippingpoint.co.uk, www.sxc.hu. p88 Scott Moore – www.typer.ca/~sgm, www.sxc.hu. p88 Wojtek Mysliwiec – www.highteckstudios.com, www.sxc.hu. p117 Jonathan Ruchti, Switzerland – www.sxc.hu. p117 Lukas – www.blogonade.de – www.sxc.hu. p117 Jonathan Ruchti, Switzerland – www.sxc.hu. p120 Pedro Simao – www.editae.com.br, www.sxc.hu. p120 Rob Owen-Wahl – www.LockStockPhotography.com, www.sxc.hu. p120 Agata Urbaniak – www.xero.prv.pl, www.sxc.hu. p124 Ove Tøpfer – www.pixelmaster.no, www.sxc.hu. p124 Ove Tøpfer – www.pixelmaster.no, www.sxc.hu. p124 Emre Nacigil – www.atolyekusadasi.com, www.sxc.hu. p128 Anna H-G – www.sxc.hu. p128 Alaa Hamed – users2.titanichost.com/alaasafei, www.sxc.hu. p128 Gunnar Brink – www.LockStockPhotography.com, www.sxc.hu. p136 Kliverap – www.sxc.hu. p136 Brandon Kettle – www.sxc.hu. p136 Johan Bolhuis – www.natuurarts.nl, www.sxc.hu. p137 Pedro Simao – www.editae.com.br, www.sxc.hu. p137 Michael Grunow – www.sxc.hu. p137 Monika M – www.sxc.hu. p145 Guenter M. Kirchweger – www.redfloor.at, www.sxc.hu. p145 Jimmy Lemon – www.jlproductions.co.uk, www.sxc.hu. p145 Torli Roberts – www.sxc.hu. p155 Nils N Kristensen – www.oadata.dk, www.sxc.hu. p155 Mateusz Kapciak – magic.4.pl, www.sxc.hu. p156 Iwan Beijes – www.beijesweb.nl www.sxc.hu. p156 Richard Dudley – www.bluegumgraphics.com.au, www.sxc.hu. p158 Andreas Just – www.justus-art.com, www.sxc.hu. p158 Gavinmusic – www.streetwisepimp.com, www.sxc.hu. p158 Cezary Porycki – wpw.24.pl, www.sxc.hu. Notepad graphic Davide Guglielmo – www.broken-arts.com, www.sxc.hu. Additional writing by Dan Cross.

cycling

SERIOUS ABOUT YOUR SPORT

Remmert Wielinga, Paul Cowcher and Tommaso Bernabei

Contents

Introduction

Inside this book there is a wealth of information for all cyclists looking to improve their times in, and enjoyment of, this great sport. I was inspired to motivate people to get the most out of their cycling experience and to pass on what I have learnt after years in the saddle and I hope this comes through in the following pages.

Most cyclists get stuck while trying to improve their performance because they don't have access to the necessary knowledge. The Internet is an endless source of information on cycling-related issues but it's often hard to piece it all together so that you have all the elements needed to become a better cyclist.

This book aims to be comprehensive, offering detailed facts and tips based on practical knowledge gained after many of years on the road. I have focused on keeping the topics straightforward without excessive 'science talk' but everything is built on a solid background and is thanks to hours and hours of research into cycling.

Cycling: serious about your sport offers you all the experience acquired throughout my professional cycling career and my time as a coach and provides you with the fundamentals for a better understanding of what is needed in this sport. Whether you are a novice, a more experienced racer, or simply a health freak trying to tone up your body, you will find this book focuses on the core skills you need to improve your cycling and will help you to keep on track with your personal targets.

The first section is dedicated to the basics of cycling because before you charge off onto the road it's always important to have some elementary knowledge of the sport.

Next up is the real world of cycling techniques, set out in a clear, graphic way. Mastering certain skills and techniques is essential for all cyclists and these include the need for a smooth pedal stroke, drafting (or slipstreaming), climbing uphill, descending, cornering, plus essentials for cold and rainy weather and cycling in the wind.

A section that outlines the principal training skills that will give you a basis for planning your endurance-training workouts follows this. No matter what your cycling goals might be, you will reap the benefits from these methods and drills.

The next section is dedicated to cross training, which is an indispensable part of a training programme for anyone who wants to get serious about their cycling.

Then there are all the facts you will need on nutrition, giving information on how to efficiently implement diet strategies.

Last but not least, there is a fully detailed description of a training programme for road cyclists, which unveils detailed professional knowledge on effectively implementing specific training methods and drills.

All this information provides a working base for you to enhance your performances if you remain committed to your cycling. We all have amazing athletic abilities and with the necessary dedication we can reach our potential.

Your dedication, together with the correct techniques and smart training tips outlined in this book, can combine to give you success in your cycling. I wish you reading pleasure, many joyful rides and wonderful achievements in this magnificent sport.

Remmert Wielinga
July 2010

the basics

Getting started

Know yourself and your limits. Recognize your strengths and weaknesses. If you are a poor sprinter, are you willing to spend time on the track to improve your speed? If you want to improve your climbing capacities, do you have the opportunity to train regularly in hilly and mountainous regions?

Stay motivated and set yourself goals and targets. As well as the physical and technical aspects, the mental side of cycling also needs your attention. Factors such as motivation, willpower, concentration, anxiety and determination have a decisive influence on whether you will realize your ambitions in cycling or not. Staying motivated to maintain your training and racing programme starts by setting the correct goals and targets. What do you want to achieve in the coming races, this season and the next?

The technique of setting proper targets is in order to maximize your targets but remain realistic. It does not make sense to always be overambitious and never succeed. Being always satisfied with results that are easy to achieve will also get you nowhere. Balancing your ambitions and reality is an important learning process in your cycling career.

Setting goals can also be related to certain aspects of racing, such as learning to ride in the middle of the bunch, participating in sprints or being involved in successful breakaways. Realizing these targets in a certain phase of the season can give you confidence in achieving your main goals.

It is likely you have faced a lack of motivation at least once in your cycling career. It may start out slowly by skipping one or two bicycle rides but it could gradually progress to the point where you are rarely riding a bicycle any more. There are a number of factors that may contribute to a loss of motivation, including disappointing performances on the road, problems in your private life, boredom, muscle soreness, or even a lack of time. Try to see these as challenges rather than barriers and apply the technique of goal setting.

• Plan your training programmes. Proper planning of your training programme is the basis of success. It ensures you have a realistic outlook and a solid strategy. The most important aspects of the design of a training programme are your physiological capabilities and training principles, such as tapering (gradually reducing your training volume and intensity), peaking (attaining your maximum potential before major competitions), and recovery (resting between sessions and seasons). The incorporation of these elements into a training programme leads to periodization. Periodization is the long-term planning and scheduling of training and racing and involves many variables, including frequency (how 'often' you train), duration (how 'long' you train for one session), volume (how 'much' you train in a given week or cycle) and intensity (how 'hard' you train at any given time). From these variables a recipe is created that will help you reach your peak for the key race(s) you are targeting. Know where you are going and how to get there.

Preparing to improve your speed

Many endurance sports do not require the extremes in physiological capabilities (eg marathoners don't need a fast sprint). However, being able to sprint is crucial to your cycling success.

Speed training shouldn't be confused with interval training. There are similarities but the difference is the length of recovery time. Interval training develops anaerobic and aerobic capacity through bursts of around 20 seconds to several minutes followed by relatively short recovery periods of a maximum of two times the length of the interval.

This training aims to improve your ability to recover from high-intensity efforts by continuously increasing and decreasing your intensity during repeated intervals. During high-intensity interval training your body will accumulate high levels of lactic acid, with your heart rate sometimes reaching 95-100 per cent of its maximum.

Speed training is used to develop rapidness and peak power. The length of the intense period shouldn't exceed 20 seconds. Speed and peak power are the key factors, not heart rate. A relatively long recovery period of six to 15 times the length of the interval should follow such sprints to ensure no lactic acid builds up in your muscles.

Your sprinting ability is influenced by reaction time and movement time. Reaction time is related to explosive power and measures how quickly you can accelerate. It is the time between the presentation of a stimulus and your subsequent response. For example, it's the time from the moment an opponent jumps in a sprint (stimulus) until you start your sprint.

Reaction time is quickest for young adults and gradually slows down with age. It can be improved with practice, up to a point, but it declines when you are fatigued. One way to improve your reaction time is to take part in group sprints. This helps you to focus on the behaviour of your competitors and gradually you will learn to react immediately when somebody jumps.

Movement time is the time needed to complete the interval, from the start of the movement to its end and is related to the top-end speed – the highest speed you can reach when sprinting. The sprint at the end of a road race will typically start with a relatively high speed, often more than 50 kph (31 mph). In this case your ability to maintain a high top-end speed is essential. But how much can you improve your sprinting ability?

You can improve but ultimately it comes down to genetics: if you don't have a high percentage (over 50 per cent) of Type IIb (fast-twitch/white) fibres, you will never become a pure sprinter. Contrary to Type I and Type IIa (red) fibres, Type IIb fibres don't have the ability to improve significantly, even under a specific training regime. Like all aspects of cycling, you need to make the most of what you have.

More about sprinting

Sprinting is something you either like or don't like. You'll notice in your early cycling years whether you can rely on your sprinting capacities or if you prefer to concentrate on endurance based areas of cycling. Some riders are genetically gifted with more fast-twitch muscle fibres (Type IIb), allowing them to develop extreme high power outputs and feel confident in bunch sprints. The riders with more slow-twitch muscle fibres however have a high resistance to fatigue and can develop excellent endurance capacities. They prefer to try to win a race by finishing alone rather than in a group sprint.

However, sprinting is critical because most races come down to a sprint – be it a small breakaway or a mass sprint at the end – it is relatively rare to see a rider win a race after a solo breakaway. Yet, many people don't pay attention to this aspect of training at all. If you're looking to improve your chances of winning, or just hoping to improve your times, incorporating a few sprint workouts on a weekly basis can help build your confidence and ability when you are sprinting.

An additional advantage is that you will improve your high-speed racing coordination. This allows you to adapt to the high-speed pace during the critical moments of the race – for example when somebody attacks or when the peloton is driving along at a rapid pace and sudden crosswinds cause the peloton to split.

Another way to improve your sprinting abilities, especially the aspect of your reaction time, is to participate in sprints in every race whenever you have a chance. If there is one area of cycling where experience counts, it's in the sprint. You have to learn from the mistakes you make at the beginning of your career to avoid making the same mistakes when it really matters later in your career.

Even if the breakaway is gone and you can't sprint for the victory anymore, you always have a possibility to improve your sprinting capacities in the race to the finish, even if it's just for fun. Another day you will be in a better position and you can then use all your sprinting experience to your advantage.

Sprinting techniques
When you prepare your jump, the position of your hands on the handlebar is very important; always place your hands down on the drops of the handlebar. This will lower your body and thus increase aerody-namics. When you start a sprint, initiate it at a very low speed, drive up and out of the saddle and bend your arms slightly as this acts as if you are running on the pedals.

Pull and push against the handlebar as you slightly move your bike from the left to the right and focus on keeping your hips vertically aligned with your bicycle; this will allow your core to create downforce on the pedals. Gradually, as speed increases after reaching your peak force, your shoulders should go forward and down, as your elbows bend because aerodynamics are becoming increasingly important.

Gearing is another critical aspect of sprinting. It should first of all coincide with your fitness level and given objective within a certain training period. Secondly, unless it's your specific objective to increase peak force, you should avoid mashing gears that are too big because it requires extremely high force peaks.

When you increase your cadence, you reduce your force output and therefore you more easily reach the maximum power level. The ideal cadence is around 130 RPM. In the final kilometres of a race, before the actual sprint, riding with a lower gear will also allow you to accelerate faster. This becomes increasingly beneficial as you have to spurt from one wheel to another in a peloton, or as you have to react to riders in a breakaway trying to escape in the final few kilometres. In either case, a lower gear allows you to respond quicker or initiate moves with more punch.

Sharpening your sprinting tactics

1. Before the race study the course map, have a look directly at the scene and pay specific attention to the last 1,000 metres (or the last 1,000 yards) of the race. Check the wind direction and anything that might cause a drop in speed like uphill stretches, corners or bottlenecks. Try to fix a reference point, knowing that from that point you are able to jump and hold it till the finish line. Always stay on the leeward side of the riders in front of you as you prepare your sprint.

2. When the race is entering the final few kilometres (or miles), try to save energy by staying out of the wind in the draft of the peloton as much as you can. It's important to stay in the first line of 20-30 riders at the front of the group. Avoid moving too much to the front though – you shouldn't waste your energy by pulling the peloton ahead while others are sitting in your wheels as you would be sapping the strength you need for the sprint. Concentrate on staying in the draft of the first riders in the peloton more and more towards the last kilometre (just over half a mile). Stay behind the riders who are setting the pace as they are the ideal 'pilots' to launch you forward for the final sprint.

3. The last point to mention is the timing of your final acceleration. You may have the fastest legs in the peloton but if your timing is off you won't necessarily win. As the finish gets closer nervous riders sprint too soon but they will not be able to maintain their speed to the finish. Don't make this mistake. Stay in the draft of the other sprinters as long as you can, then find or make an opening and only start your final jump when you are sure it's the moment to power to the finish line. Always continue to sprint through the line and never stop pedalling before – the race does not finish until you've crossed the line!

Power and speed

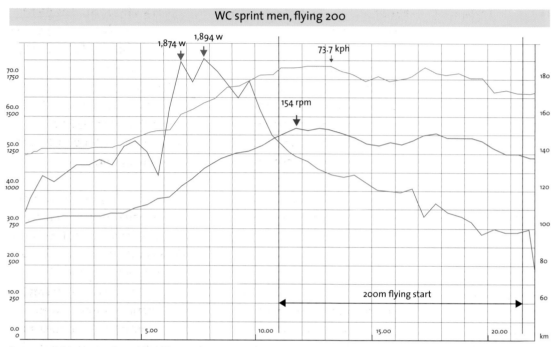

WC sprint men, flying 200

Power (watt) in green • Speed (kph) in purple   Cadence (rpm) in blue

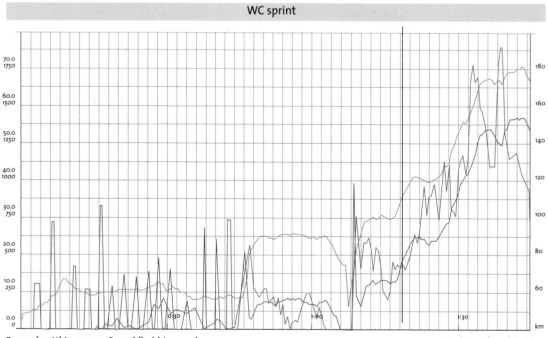

WC sprint

Power (watt) in green • Speed (kph) in purple   Cadence (rpm) in blue

Example of a men's individual sprint

What kind of speeds and powers do these riders hit? Let's take a look at a file from a rider who won a World Cup in this event (although this file is from a different World Cup). First, let's look at the flying 200m qualification ride (see graph opposite top).

1. From the start of the big effort until the finish line he took about 22 seconds, with an average power of 1184W over that time.
2. Peak power reached was 1894W, 3.5 seconds before the start of the 200 metres.
3. Average power during the 200m was 975W, at an average speed of 70.95 kph (44.09 mph).
4. Average cadence for roughly 10.5 seconds 200 metres was 148 RPM.

You can see that the biggest effort was made just before the beginning of the 200 metres to get the speed and cadence up to their peak before the effort began.

In the match sprints, the profile looks quite different, depending on what tactics were used. However, there is always a sprint for the finish. Let's have a look at one of the match sprints from the same day as the qualification ride.

1. The speed for about the first 100 metres was around 10 kph (six mph) or less... very slow.
2. The speed went up a bit for the next 100 metres to about 25 kph (16 mph) after an effort of 575W.
3. The rider slowed right down again and then there was a larger but still intermittent effort that

took the speed to about 55 kph (34 mph).
4. The rider 'jumped' from there, making a big effort of 1781W (still not maximal for this rider), taking the speed up to 67 kph (42 mph) and the cadence up to about 148 RPM.
5. The final burst happened about 100 metres from the finish line, with the rider hitting 1898W and 70.7 kph (43.9 mph).

The powers and speeds these riders hit are incredible, but what is most impressive is their control over their efforts and their bike. Track sprinters have some of the best bicycle skills around, and usually maintain control of their bike even when there is contact with the other rider at speeds around 70 kph (43 mph).

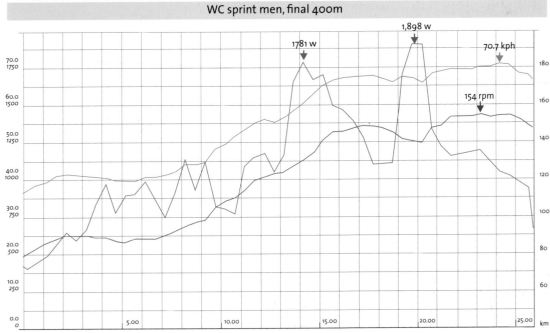

Power (watt) in green • Speed (kph) in purple   Cadence (rpm) in blue   Courtesy of www.srm.com

The principles of training

The **SPORT** principles of training are aimed at helping you understand the training process and allowing you to plan your training so you see a steady upward progression in results.

Specificity – making sure your training is specific to what you are hoping to achieve. Simply put, don't spend all your time doing sprint training sets if you want to improve your long-distance cycling!

Progression – the body adapts to increased training loads and this will result in improved fitness levels and competitive performance.

Overload – training at a level that will push you. If you are always training at the same intensity and at the same speed you will not see the progression you would hope for. You need to be constantly overloading your muscles and cardio respiratory system to improve your strength and fitness level.

Reversibility – if you don't train or you decrease your intensity then you will see your fitness levels drop and as a consequence so will your overall performance. If you are unwell and are unable to train for an extended period then you will notice a reduced performance level when you start training again.

Tedium – keeping the training interesting. If you find yourself getting bored then you are less likely to want to train and your motivation levels will automatically drop, which can lead to a reduced effort level and even the likelihood of skipping training sessions. This will lead to Reversibility occurring.

When you start to plan your training programme you can use the FITT principles to work towards SPORT. For instance, to make sure that the SPORT principles of Progression and Overload are always occurring you can increase the Frequency

of your training sessions, the Intensity of each session or the Time you spend training. To stop Reversibility occurring rapidly you reduce Intensity if feeling sick. To avoid the SPORT principle of Tedium you can change the Type of training methods you are using. It is advisable that you only change one aspect of the training at a time rather than changing everything otherwise it can be too much for your body and may lead to an injury occurring.

Frequency – how often you train.

Intensity – intensity you train at.

Time – how long you train for.

Type – which training methods you are using.

Sleep, food and fluid

Getting your work-to-rest ratio right is crucial, as an imbalance will lead to over-training, which may result in a decreased performance in training and racing, as well as an increased chance of injury. Put simply: rest is as important as the training itself. As you get fitter you will be able to train longer as long as you keep getting quality rest.

- Set a schedule: be strict in your sleep regime. Sleep and wake at the same time every day including weekends and try to get at least eight hours of rest. Disrupting this schedule may lead to insomnia. 'Catching up' by sleeping extra on weekends makes it harder to wake up early on Monday morning because it re-sets your sleep cycles.

- Exercise: daily exercise will help you sleep, although a workout too close to your bedtime may disrupt your sleep. For maximum benefit try to get your exercise about five to six hours before going to bed.

- Avoid caffeine, nicotine, and alcohol: don't take these stimulants close to your bedtime. Remember there is caffeine in coffee, chocolate, soft drinks, non-herbal teas, diet drugs and some pain relievers. Don't smoke a cigarette before going to bed as nicotine goes straight to the sleep centres of your brain and will result in a bad night's rest. Alcohol can decrease the time required to fall asleep. However, too much alcohol consumed within an hour of bedtime will deprive you of deep sleep and REM sleep (the sleep that rejuvenates your body the best) and it will keep you in the lighter stages of sleep.

- Relax before bed: reading, listening to music, having sex, taking a warm bath, can all make it easier to fall asleep. You can train yourself to associate certain activities with sleep and make them part of your bedtime ritual. If you can't get to sleep, don't just lie in bed – relax and do something else (like the previously mentioned activities) until you feel tired.

- Control your room temperature: make sure that you sleep in a room that is cool – 18-19 °C (64-66 °F) with 65 per cent of humidity is ideal – as well as dark and quiet.

So train hard and rest well. Nutrition can help supplement your training by giving you the right balance of energy to train and the proteins, vitamins and minerals to help you recover. If you are not getting the right levels of carbohydrates, proteins, fats and vitamins you will quickly feel tired in training and will fail to recover properly, which can lead to fatigue and maybe illness and injury. Hydration is critical, as the body has to be topped up to perform at its peak. Even a one per cent drop in hydration levels will impair your performance. Get used to taking on fluids.

Equipment

The correct position on the bicycle

If you want to get the most out of your cycling then finding your correct position on the bicycle is paramount. Cycling comfort and efficiency begin with a bicycle that fits. Getting your position correct means you are able to produce more power efficiently without working any muscles unnecessarily. Correct positioning of hands, feet and body are essential for success and avoiding injury. If you have back, neck, shoulder or knee pain, saddle sores or finger numbness, then your bicycle probably doesn't fit you.

We are all very different, each of us with different sizes of arms, legs, torsos and other parts of the body. All these factors must be evaluated when you seek to find your correct position on the bicycle. The following are some basic recommendations to provide you with a nearly perfect set-up. With experience you can then slightly adjust this position to meet your own requirements.

Frame size

To start in getting the right bicycle size, stand over the frame with your bare feet flat on the ground. A correctly sized road bicycle frame should give two and a half to five centimetres (one to two inches) of clearance between the top tube of the frame and your crotch. A more precise method to calculate the frame size is the formula: inseam length x 0.64.

The result of this formula is unequivocally correct but it's important to realize it pertains to traditional frame geometry. This is the conventional way of measuring the frame size 'centre to centre', which indicates the length of the seat tube from the centre of the bottom bracket to the centre of the seat lug (the point at which the centre line of the seat tube and the centre line of the top tube cross each other). Other ways to measure the size of a frame are:

Centre to top

Centre to top indicates the length of the seat tube from the centre of the bottom bracket to the top side of the seat lug. As a rule, this frame size should equal the centre-to-centre size, plus 15 to 20 millimetres (about three quarters of an inch).

Compact frame size

Many bicycle manufacturers specify the frame size of their sloping/

compact frames according to the length of the seat tube, measured centre to centre as well as from centre to top. The frame size is then usually not specified as a numeric value but is simply expressed as 'small, medium, or large'. The problem with this way of measuring is that it turns out to be complicated to precisely calculate an ideal frame size, unless the manufacturer also provides the traditional centre-to-centre measurement in addition to the compact specification.

Choose a frame with the right seat-tube angle

The most important angle on a frame is the seat-tube angle. This is the angle made by the seat tube and an imaginary horizontal line. It significantly influences the saddle set-back position and therefore is of vital importance to determine the seat angle before buying the frame.

The seat-tube angle is related to the length of your upper leg (femur). A standard frame angle measures 72 to 75 degrees and allows a cyclist with an average-femur length to position the knee straight above the pedal axle with only small adjustments in fore and aft movement of the saddle. The longer your femur, the smaller the seat-tube angle and the farther back the saddle will have to be positioned.

Adjusting the contact points on your bicycle

On a bicycle, the weight of your body is supported at three locations:

- The pedals support your feet.
- The saddle supports your butt.
- The handlebars support your hands.

Ensure each is correctly positioned as described below.

Shoe cleats

Before you start to adjust other aspects of your position on the bicycle you first have to properly fit the shoe cleats. To maximize the efficiency of your 'ankling' and to avoid knee pain later on, the cleats should be adjusted so the ball of your foot is directly above the centre line of the pedal axle. This will allow you to realize optimal power transmission and the risk of the well-known burning feet sensation will considerably abate and in some cases even disappear completely.

Adjusting the saddle height

Once you have chosen the right frame and you've properly fitted the shoe cleats it's time to look at the height of the saddle as it is the most important aspect of positioning on your bicycle. The saddle height affects the muscle activity of your legs. If the saddle is placed too high you run the risk of over-stretching your muscles and when the saddle is

placed too low the pressure on your quadriceps might become disproportionately high.

The correct saddle height enables your muscles to work optimally in the longitudinal reach and you will be able to maximize your power. You measure the saddle height from the heart of the bottom bracket to the upper part of the saddle in line with the seat post. To calculate your saddle height you have to know your inseam length. Your inseam length is measured as follows:

1. Stand straight up on your bare feet with your heels, back and head against a wall.
2. Position the inside of your feet approximately 15 to 20 centimetres (six to eight inches) apart.
3. Put a tube (eg a plastic bottle) with a diameter of three and a half to seven and a half centimetres (about one and a half to three inches) against your crotch, exerting the same pressure as your saddle would.
4. The edge of the tube should be horizontal and flush with the wall.
5. Ask a friend to draw a small line on the wall where the tube reaches its highest point.

The formula to measure the optimal saddle height = inseam length x 0.88.

Note: this saddle height calculation is based on Look Keo pedals and other pedals have a different stack height (see Table 1). This is the distance from the top of the cleat to the centre of the pedal axle. The closer your foot is positioned to the axle the more efficiently power is transmitted to your bicycle. When you change pedals your foot might be closer to the axle. The lower the stack height, the lower the saddle height. As an example, 87.5 (inseam length) x 0.88 = 77cm saddle height with Look Keo pedals (stack height 17.1mm). When you then switch to, let's say, Shimano SPD SL pedals (stack height 13.7mm) you should decrease your saddle height according to the difference in stack height between the two pedals. This is 17.1mm - 13.7mm = 3.4mm, giving a new saddle height of 76.6cm.

If you need to radically change your saddle height then make the adjustments gradually so your body has time to adapt! If you are currently used to a saddle height that is off by a lot, then adjust the saddle by 2 millimetres (a fraction of an inch) per week.

Fore and aft position of the saddle

The forward and backward adjustment (fore and aft position) of the saddle plays an important role as well. If your saddle is placed too far backwards it will result in an exaggerated lowering of your heel when your pedal reaches its maximum force angle at three o'clock (See Smooth pedal stroke pages 38-41). If, on the other hand, the saddle is placed too far forwards your toes point down too much. This results in a loss of power and efficiency. The following method allows you to properly adjust the fore and aft position.

First, get seated comfortably and click your cycling shoes (with properly mounted cleats) into the pedals while the crank arms and shoes are horizontal to the ground (ask a friend to check). Be sure the pressure in the front and rear tyres are equal and, even more importantly, the ground must be level!

Then drop a plumb line from the front of your forward kneecap. It should directly cross the forward pedal's axle. When the line drops in front or behind the pedal's axle you have to move the saddle forwards or backwards along its rails as needed.

The rails under the saddle have a margin of about 55 millimetres (2.2 inches) to move forwards and backwards. After any fore and aft adjustment you should recheck the saddle height. Moving the saddle forwards means you must slightly lower the saddle as well, while moving the saddle backwards means you must slightly increase the saddle height.

Your saddle should be level to support your full body weight and allow you to move around on the saddle when necessary. In almost no case is it a good idea to ride with a saddle that's tilted up at the front.

Too much upward tilt can result in pressure points. As you slide forward you are essentially pushing your most delicate parts into the nose of the saddle if it's up at the front which may lead to health problems later on. A downward-tilted saddle can make you slide forward while riding and put extra pressure on your arms, hands and knees, which can ultimately lead to injury. You can easily check the saddle's level by placing a spirit level along the longitudinal axis of the saddle.

Stem extension

The measurement that most influences your upper-body position is the combination of handlebar extension and top-tube length, or the so-called 'reach'. In a standard off-the-shelf frame the length of the top tube is correctly related to the length of the seat tube and correlates to the upper body measurements of a cyclist of average size who would need that frame size.

To determine a proper stem extension, place your hands in the drop position (or on the tops of the brake levers) while you are comfortably seated in your saddle with your elbows slightly bent (ground must be level!). In this position the front wheel's hub should then be obscured by the middle section of your handlebar. If proper top tube/stem length combination cannot be achieved with a 105-135 millimetres (4.1-5.3 inches) stem, try a larger frame.

It is clear that a correct aerodynamic position and a comfortable position of the torso do not always go hand in hand. Depending on your anatomy, flexibility and the discipline you engage in, the reach could be longer for better aerodynamics and higher speeds, or it may need to be shorter for back or neck comfort and improved efficiency uphill. If your reach to the handlebar is wrong, use stem length to correct it, not fore/aft saddle position.

Stem height
Start with the top of the stem about four to five centimetres (about one and a half to two inches) below the top of the saddle. This should give you comfortable access to the

Table 1

Type of Pedal	Stack height in mm (in)
Look PP 296	22.0 (0.86)
Look CX 6	21.3 (0.84)
Campagnolo Pro Fit	20.5 (0.81)
Look Keo (used as reference in formula)	17.1 (0.67)
Time Equipe (3-hole mounting)	16.5 (0.65)
Shimano SL	13.7 (0.54)
Time RSX	12.5 (0.49)
Time RXS / RXE	12.5 (0.49)
Shimano SPDR	12.0 (0.47)
Time Impact (3-hole mounting)	12.2 (0.48)
Time Impact (4-hole mounting)	11.5 (0.45)
Speed Play (3-hole mounting)	11.5 (0.45)
Time Equipe (4-hole mounting)	8.8 (0.35)

Table 2

Inseam length in cm (in)	Length of cranks in mm (in)
74-80 (29.1-31.5)	170 (6.69)
81-86 (31.9-33.8)	172.5 (6.79)
87-93 (34.3-36.6)	175 (6.89)

Table 3 – Measurements

FH	Frame Height
TT	Top Tube
SA	Seat Angle
SH	Saddle Height
FA	Fore and Aft
SE	Stem Extension
SH	Stem Height
SL	Stem Length
HW	Handlebar Width
CL	Crank Length

handlebars. As time goes by you could lower the stem by another two to three centimetres (about an inch) to help your aerodynamic position. Going lower than this improves your aerodynamics but restrains breathing and your lower back or neck might start complaining. In general, the higher your stem, the better you will climb and the lower your stem, the more aerodynamic you will be. Most riders position their stems too low and rarely take advantage of the drop position of their handlebars.

Handlebar width

For a road bicycle, the handlebar width should correspond with the width of your shoulders. Handlebars that are too wide increase the frontal surface area and lead to a loss of aerodynamics. Contrary to general belief, narrow handlebars do not result in a loss of oxygen intake, but they lead to more nervous steering than wide handlebars and therefore the bicycle becomes less comfortable to ride.

Crank length

The great majority of cyclists use crank lengths of 170-175 millimetres (6.7-6.9 inches). Longer crank arms allow you to push larger gears at a lower cadence, while shorter arms promote high cadences with smaller gears. Sprinters, who need explosive power, are used to shorter cranks, while time-trial specialists and riders with good climbing abilities favour longer cranks. See Table 2 for an indication of the crank arm length to use under typical riding conditions in most disciplines.

Elliptical chain rings

It's difficult to imagine what could be wrong with ordinary round chain rings. After all, numerous cyclists worldwide have ridden millions of kilometres on round rings. Furthermore, every professional race in the world has been won on round rings and top riders have demonstrated over and over again that it's certainly possible to produce extraordinary power outputs very efficiently while using them.

However, human physiology is not necessarily designed for pedalling in perfect even circles. Measurements of force output demonstrate that a rider is substantially stronger while pushing down through the middle of the pedalling stroke than at the top and bottom of the rotation. Many cyclists spend years combating this and perfecting technique to drive through these so-called 'dead spots' in an effort to maximize pedalling efficiency.

The idea behind non-round rings is to use mechanical rather than physiological means to improve your pedalling efficiency and/or power output by carefully varying the effective chain ring size throughout the pedal stroke. The rings are generally designed so you are pushing a bigger gear during the downstroke, when the power output is greatest, and a smaller gear at the top and bottom of the stroke to speed the transition through the dead spots, where power output is greatly reduced.

Using the example of O'symetrics (one of the manufacturers of elliptical chain rings, which has been used by among others, Bradley Wiggins), the standard outer road ring has 52 teeth, but because of its elliptical shape it is effectively a 56-tooth ring in the power stroke, and a 48-toother as the rider's feet pass through the dead spots.

This results, the manufacturer claims, depending on the level of effort, in a five to 15 per cent power output increase and a three per cent increase in speed compared to regular round rings. Furthermore, there are some less quantifiable advantages, such as reduced knee strain resulting from the reduced effort in the high-stress dead zones, more consistent power output, and improved traction in off-road situations, particularly at low cadences.

technique & tactics
// SHARPER // SMARTER // MORE EFFICIENT

The basics

Most of us just want to get out on our bicycle and ride. There's nothing wrong with that – after all we love cycling. But to get the most out of your riding, to improve your efficiency, to conserve your energy, and most importantly to improve your race times, you need to spend time on improving your technique. Just a small amount of time spent on a few aspects of your cycling technique will yield results for you. Keep fine-tuning the techniques you learn, using everything you can to your advantage. In top races the smallest advantage gained through better technique can mean the difference between a winner and someone back in the pack.

Most importantly you need to ensure you have, and can maintain, a smooth pedal stroke and eliminate the 'dead spots' at the top and bottom of your pedal stroke. Concentrate on applying an even force throughout the turn of the pedal stroke, both pushing down and pulling up, thus reducing inefficiency of movement. You must always feel a comfortable rhythm in your 360-degree rotation and not feel like you are fighting the bicycle. Once you have achieved this you will pedal without thinking, leaving you to concentrate on improving other aspects of your cycling.

Improving your technique means you can also take on even the most daunting of hill climbs with a feeling of strength. You will also find that you gain confidence as you descend and corner at greater and greater speeds.

Valuable time can be saved on hills – both going up and coming down. Improve your technique and this time is all yours. And no cyclist who wants to see an improvement in his times can ignore the role of riding in a group and drafting, crucial to conserving energy you can use later in the race. Your confidence, whether it is on hills, corners or in riding in large groups, will come from having a good basic technique in all of these situations. Once you trust your technique you will see continuing improvements in all aspects of your cycling.

The weather also plays a role in cycling so it's important you learn to adapt your technique accordingly and apply those in the wet and the wind. Of course, we all wish the weather conditions were perfect all the time but they are not. Improved technique will mean you will no longer groan at the sight of dark clouds or the feeling of wind in the air. And there emerges another benefit of better technique: once you have worked at it your motivation for taking on difficult situations will rise. There really will be nothing to fear anymore.

Many elements go together in making you a better cyclist – training, nutrition, natural talent to name just a few – but you must constantly strive to improve your technique and keep working at maintaining it so you do not fall back into bad habits.

Smooth pedal stroke

1 Concentrate on 'pulling up' during the third and fourth quadrants of the stroke (from six to 12 o'clock), lifting your heel for extra pull.

2 Concentrate on 'pushing down' during the first quadrant of the stroke (from 12 to three o'clock).

3 Aim to move through the dead spots of the pedal cycle – 12 o'clock and six o'clock – as smoothly as possible.

A smooth pedal stroke is a critical aspect of the forward driving of your bicycle. Imagine the difference between an exhausted cyclist hitting his pedals as if he's hammering them down and the powerful cyclist who caresses his pedals by turning them around smoothly and forcefully. The difference in pedalling efficiency is enormous. In the history of professional cycling we have seen great cyclists successfully applying different pedalling techniques.

Jacques Anquetil became famous not only because of his achievements but also as the cyclist who set the benchmark for pedalling efficiency. Anquetil had a unique pedalling style, which held many secrets. He did biomechanically what the best engineers have tried in vain to do by mechanical means, which was to eliminate the entire dead spot area of the pedal stroke thanks to a phenomenal use of his ankles. His pedalling technique allowed him to extend the effective, profitable phase of his pedalling and therefore decreasing the force peak of each pedal stroke.

Engineers since have been studying the biomechanical and physical factors involved in pedalling. Very few, though, have been able to find a mechanical solution by developing a product that improves the pedalling efficiency. There are, however, some chain rings available on the global bicycle component market, which aim to improve pedalling efficiency significantly (see The basics on page 32).

Biomechanists studying the pedalling efficiency look at the different forces a cyclist applies on the pedals to identify and teach pedalling technique. They differentiate two different force components that influence the pedalling efficiency.

The first component is the tangential force component that transmits rotational force to the crank arm and is thus a component of effective force as it is powering the bicycle ahead.

The second component, the radial force component, acts parallel to the crank arm along the surface of the pedal and therefore only tends to alter the shape by 'lengthening' or even 'deforming' the crank arm and, producing no rotary force, which represents an ineffective force component.

With regard to pedalling technique, the extent to which these two forces are applied on the pedals will result in a more (or less) efficient pedal stroke. Applying more tangential force to the crank and reducing the radial force is the most effective way to increase your pedalling efficiency. The result is increased torque, which is the product of the tangential force component and the crank-arm length.

Although you won't notice it while riding, the applied force on the pedal throughout the pedal stroke changes continuously, both in intensity and direction. A pedal stroke consists of four quadrants: the first quadrant downward and forward, the second downward and backward, the third upward and backward, and the fourth quadrant upward and forward returning to the starting point.

During the pedal stroke you will be confronted with the so-called 'dead spot', or the top dead centre of the pedal stroke. Analysis with force-measuring devices have showed that when the pedals are on the top with the cranks in a vertical position, the applied force on the pedal is close to zero. During the first quadrant, after going through the dead top centre, you gradually increase your force output until the crank arm reaches the three o'clock position. At this point you attain the peak force of the pedal stroke.

In the second quadrant, from the three o'clock position until the dead bottom centre of the pedal rotation, the force on the pedal is decreasing significantly. During the third and fourth quadrants (from six to 12 o'clock) of the stroke the weight of your foot and leg apply a negative force, which is slowing down the upward movement of the pedals and thus causing a counter torque.

But what can you do to improve your pedalling? The answer is not simple because the complex web of physical and mechanical variables makes it difficult for cyclists, coaches, manufacturers and scientists to apply biomechanics to cycling. But there are certain factors that are adjustable and therefore can help improve your performance and pedalling efficiency.

The muscles you use to pedal and your ankle movement are interrelated, with adjustable mechanical factors like the frame geometry, saddle height, crank length, type of pedals, foot position, type of chain rings (circular or non-circular) etc. A proper bicycle fit, along with correct cleat positioning is essential to optimizing the efficiency of your pedal stroke (see The basics on pages 26-33).

To optimize your pedal efficiency you need to get the maximum

benefit from your ankle movement. Optimal ankle movement or 'ankling' consists of progressively pushing down through the top of your stroke and pulling up at the bottom. The action involves a lowering of the heel as the downward force of the pedals takes place and a lifting of the heel as the pedal begins the upward movement of its revolution.

The key point of ankling is to always stay focused on the leverage of your crank arms by the upward pulling of the pedals during the recovery phase of the pedal motion. This technique enables the application of constant pressure upon the pedals throughout the revolution, eliminating, to a certain extent, the dead spots at the upper and lower points of the cycle.

The result is a pedal stroke that requires less peak muscle contraction, which spreads the load over the muscles (engaging more calf muscles) and promoting a smooth, efficient style. You will be able to produce more power with less difficulty. This technique can be applied during climbing with low-rotation speed. However, during high-speed sections with high cadences riders cannot think about individual strokes and revert to what comes naturally to them.

Typically cyclists will apply different ankle movements while pedalling. Depending on your flexibility and basic biomechanics, you may use a high heel action and or a low heel action. Also your speed and cadence have a large influence: the faster your cadence, the more difficult it will be to keep control over your pedalling technique. The downwards force on the pedals and the muscle contraction will be so quick in a sprint at 140 RPM that you won't be able to manage your pedalling technique.

You'll notice that while sprinting on the flat with such a high cadence your toes tend to point down significantly. When you're spinning (pedalling fast with little resistance) you don't need to generate much power and your foot favours the least possible movement at the ankle, thus maintaining a vertical angle to your lower leg. But as you pedal more slowly, perhaps needing more power for a climb or to push through a headwind, modifying the angle of your foot at various points of the pedal stroke can increase your power. The low heel technique is important in hill climbing while sitting back on the saddle and you'll notice an improvement in your climbing abilities once you master this technique.

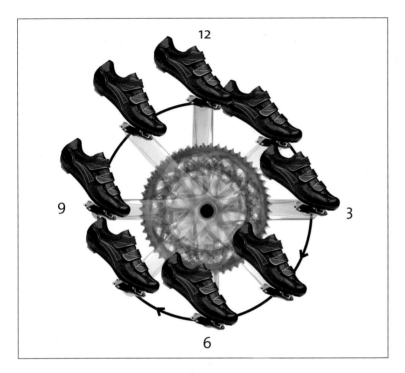

This illustrates the ideal ankling technique for riding on the flat (90+ RPM). Notice the strong 'unrolling' motion between three and six o'clock and the higher ankle/heel during the complete pedal stroke compared to the technique for riding uphill. Toes should be pointed more downwards and this effect will be even more visible when increasing your cadence. This is an automatic tendency so don't try to force your natural ankle movement. You may end up injuring yourself if you attempt to change the natural heel height of your pedal stroke. Remember: you should try to develop ankling within the bounds of your basic pedalling movement, always respecting your natural abilities.

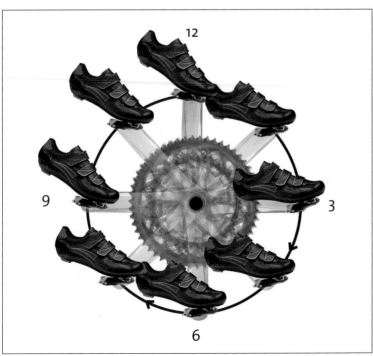

This illustrates the ideal ankling technique for riding uphill (ie 60-90 RPM). The ankling pattern will vary from an almost horizontal foot position at one o'clock to slightly heel down at three o'clock. The heel down lowering should then reduce progressively until your pedal reaches the lowest position at six o'clock and gets the toes back by the time the pedal reaches the five o'clock position. When the pedal reaches the upstroke (from six o'clock to 12 o'clock) of the pedal motion (the so-called recovery phase) your toes should slightly point downwards and your heel move up with a maximum toes-down position at eight o'clock of the pedal stroke.

Drafting

1 Drafting will save you up to 20 to 30 per cent of your energy. Tuck in close to benefit.

2 Ride at a comfortable distance from others when first riding in a group. About 50cm to 70cm (20in to 28in) is a good starting point.

3 Focus on the group as a whole rather than only on the rider in front of you.

Drafting is when you ride behind another rider or in a group of riders to get the benefit of the reduced airflow, so that you are working less and conserving energy for later in the race. Essentially you are getting a 20 to 30 per cent advantage of drafting the riders in front of you as compared to when you are riding alone or in the front of a group. If you are in a bigger peloton, your benefit can be even greater than this.

Be aware that a group takes on its own personality. Unlike the dynamics of most groups, the smaller the group, the less one individual's actions is likely to have an effect on the group as a whole. As a group grows larger an individual's actions has a greater effect on that group. So, one error from someone in a small group can be easily overcome by the others by them making small adjustments in their riding but that same mistake in a large group is likely to have a knock-on effect because they are tightly packed and have less room for manoeuvre. Making an error in a larger group therefore increases the risk of causing an accident.

To get comfortable with riding in groups, start by riding in a small group first. A group of five or six people is ideal to learn the basic

techniques needed when riding in a peloton. Start by maintaining a distance from the other cyclists that makes you feel comfortable. When you are not acquainted with riding in a group this distance can mean keeping your front wheel anywhere from 50cm to 70cm (20 to 28 in) from the rear wheel of the rider immediately in front of you. The distance from your shoulders to the shoulders of those either side of you will be about the same to start with, but again, use the 'comfortable' rule. Over time, as your confidence and

technique improves, this distance can get closer. Professional cyclists can ride at high speeds while rubbing shoulders and almost touching the wheel of the cyclist in front of them, but this takes a rare talent and years of practice.

What you need to learn to do is to be able to gauge the distance of the wheel in front of you by focusing on the rider(s) beyond the bicycle that is/are riding ahead of you. It is the same as when driving a car – you judge the position of your vehicle by looking forwards and using your peripheral vision, not focusing only on the front of your car. In this way you are going to learn where your bike is in relation to the other riders in the peloton.

You should always avoid staring down at the wheel right in front of you, or your own wheel, because that can be very dangerous. You need to be looking ahead of you. Another tip, especially when you start riding closer to the other riders and closing the gap, is to always ride slightly to the left or the right side of the

✓ Get close to benefit from drafting.

✗ Not too close to avoid accidents.

✓ Keep your eyes looking forward.

✗ Don't look down at your front wheel.

✓ Exit the peloton from the side.

✗ Avoid sudden movements or braking.

✓ Practice peloton riding in a small group to start with.

✗ Don't move into bigger groups until you have experience.

wheel of the person in front of you and not follow in a direct straight line. In that way you have the ability to move gently to either side according to the slight movements of the other rider. This is especially important as you will need more room for manoeuvre as the peloton moves into a corner or a cyclist looks to change his position because he wants to exit the peloton.

If, for whatever reason, you want to exit a peloton, you need to be aware that your movement will have an effect on the group. Pelotons are fluid and constantly moving around as well as forwards but you need to gradually make your way to the side before exiting. If there is enough space for you to move into, your change in direction will make your intentions clear, otherwise a small signal, with either your hand or eyes, will be enough to alert your fellow riders.

Towards the end of a race top racers are less likely to let someone move out of a peloton so easily (especially in the front section) as they are all fighting to secure their position. At this stage, jostling for open space and the front is often forced with the use of arms and shoulders and the bicycle position. This jostling also occurs as critical parts of

the race approach (such as a steep climb, a sector of cobblestones or an area of crosswind). At stages like this the peloton is likely to get strung out and riders don't want to be left at the back or they will need to expend a lot of energy fighting their way back to the front later.

These simple techniques will help you to avoid crashes if somebody suddenly brakes or slows down. The more you practice these techniques the more you will start to feel at ease in the peloton and the more you will be efficient in saving necessary energy that can help you improve your times.

4 Space will constantly keep opening up in the peloton. Keep moving into it to maintain your position.

5 Align yourself to the left or right of the rear wheel of the rider directly in front of you and not directly behind.

6 Know the race course and maintain a good peloton position at places on the course that are likely to force the group to stretch out.

Hill climbing

1 Approach the hills as a challenge not a problem and your motivation levels will rise.

2 When riding out of the saddle keep centred so the power is pushing down through the pedals and don't pull hard on the handlebars.

3 Before you hit the steepest part of the climb make sure you have already set up your chosen gear.

Most people see a climb as a huge obstacle and their motivation drops when they look up. But hills are an integral part of training and racing and you will need to learn to embrace them with confidence if you want to start reducing your race times. Hill climbing may never become your favourite part of cycling but with good technique, mental approach and fitness levels you will discover there is nothing to fear from a hill or mountain climb. You will even start to enjoy the challenge over time and when a climb becomes a challenge your motivation levels to take on the climb will rise as you approach it.

As you approach the hill always prepare your gears before you hit the steepest grades. Obviously if the climb starts with a low gradient you can enter it in higher gears and adjust your gears gradually as the gradient increases. But do not attack the steepest part of a climb with a big gear that results in your pedal cadence grinding to a halt – maintain your momentum and keep turning your legs.

When you are on the flat you will have to shift to the smaller ring in the front before the transition to the hill. As you shift and allow the chain to drop to the smaller ring, continue pedalling but gently

relieve the pressure on the pedals so the chain doesn't drop off onto the inside. Relieving this pressure is very difficult if you are struggling in a high gear on a steep gradient because of the pressure the chain is under and you may be forced to come to a virtual standstill to be able to relieve that pressure enough to change to the correct gear. This may sound like a beginner's mistake but even professionals sometimes find themselves facing a long, steep climb from a standing start because of a poor gear change. There is nothing worse than having to dismount on a climb and having

to turn your pedals manually to change to the correct gear.

Assuming you have shifted success-fully going into the hill, you must then select the appropriate gear from the cassette for the gradient of the hill. Riding uphill is all about managing your effort and not your speed so consider that when choosing your gear. It's important to get to the top of the climb within your capabilities rather than trying to force yourself into keeping up a certain speed you may not be able to maintain. If you are approaching the hill at a high speed you clearly shouldn't expect to maintain this high speed until the top of the hill. So keep focusing on managing your effort, not your speed. This will help you pace yourself up the hill. When you use a heart-rate monitor or a device that measures your wattage output you can control your effort more accurately.

Don't attempt to win points by conquering a hill in a high gear – it is more effective to maintain a higher pedal cadence in a lower gear. One of the reasons why Lance Armstrong became a Tour de France champion is because he was able to spin his legs with a high cadence with lower gears.

An optimal pedal cadence to maintain speed and for maximum energy efficiency depends on the abilities and fitness of each individual rider but is around 60-90 RPM. Any lower than 60 RPM and you are significantly increasing the force (and energy) you are applying to each pedal stroke and any higher than 90 RPM you are increasing your heart rate (and using your energy) without any associated benefit.

Another important part of hill climbing is the positioning of your hands on the handlebar. Generally, the tops of the handlebar are used

for riding uphill, especially if you are at the front of a group or if you are riding alone, as this will naturally force you to straighten up, therefore opening up your lungs and giving you more air for the climb. As you climb you must relax your body and breathe steadily. Tensing up will affect your breathing patterns.

If you are riding uphill in the middle of a group then place your hands on the shifters as this allows you to access your gears and brakes if you need to react to a change in the speed or rhythm of the group. Another advantage of placing your hands on the shifters is that this is the right position for when you decide to get out of the saddle. If the hill is getting steep this will give you leverage, allowing you to transmit more power on the pedals as you move the handlebars slightly to the left and to the right.

Avoid leaning forward to keep your power driving down the centre of the bicycle through the pedals. Riding out of the saddle will increase your heart rate and give you more power but use this sparingly to burst through steep sections or to change the working muscles briefly.

Your foot position is also an important aspect when you

are climbing. For most people, the foot should be flat when the crank position is horizontal and that foot position should be maintained throughout the pedal stroke. You shouldn't change the flexion between your foot and your shin too much. Some people have a tendency to ride with their toes down (like the legendary cyclist Jacques Anquetil), others with the heel down and the toes up (like Eddy Merckx), but the best position for most people is flat. Whatever your natural tendency or preference, try to keep that same angle throughout your pedal stroke.

✓ See a hill as a challenge.

✗ Do not fear a hill.

✓ Ride at a pedal cadence of 60-90 RPM.

✗ Avoid gears that are too low for this range.

✓ Relax your body as you climb.

✗ Don't tense or your breathing will be affected.

✓ Stay centred over the bicycle when out of the saddle.

✗ Avoid leaning forward.

4 When riding in a group put your hands on the shifters so you can manoeuvre the bicycle and brake quickly if needed.

5 Position your hands on top of the handlebars if you have space to ride, such as when you are leading a group or riding alone.

6 The key to climbing is to manage your effort not your speed. Don't get fixated on maintaining a particular speed.

Cornering

1 Concentrate on keeping your weight centred through the bicycle.

2 Push forward with your inside hand as you enter the turn.

3 Push down on your outside pedal as you enter the turn.

Steering around a corner is not simply a matter of turning the handlebars. This technique is fine when used at low speeds but when professionals or advanced riders think about steering a bike they will talk of another technique: the counter-steering method.

This is the technique you need to master when cornering on a downhill stretch at higher speeds or riding fast in a peloton. At a high speed you can't just steer through a turn because your bicycle will skip out and you will not be able to lean into it.

So, as you increase your speeds on your bicycle, you must use the method of counter steering. As you start to approach a turn, let's say a right turn, you need to turn your outside pedal down (the left pedal in this case). You then apply pressure with your foot on your outside pedal and gently push forward with your inside hand (in this case your right hand).

This turns the handlebars very slightly in the opposite direction and causes your bicycle to create the necessary lean to initiate the turn. Avoid putting too much pressure on your handlebars with your hands as you will be forcing it and this will cause you to slip,

especially during wet weather conditions. Trust the technique to corner you successfully.

Counter-steering allows your bike to fall into position naturally and to get into the correct lean position to make the turn. While you push your outside pedal down you have to think about your core and your weight on the saddle, concentrating on driving straight through the bicycle and the bottom bracket through to the ground. It's important to stay focused on maintaining the weight of your body through

the centre. Anyone who has been skiing may recognize this technique, as keeping your weight through the centre of the body is similar for keeping control and balance.

As you approach a corner you need to select the line that allows you to maintain speed as much as possible. The line should take you from the outside of the corner as you approach, then to the inside on its apex and swinging back to the outside again as you leave the corner.

Obviously, when riding at low speed, such as when you are climbing a hill, the counter-steering method is not applicable.

✓ Use the counter-steering method to corner at speeds.

✗ Do not simply turn the handlebars.

✓ Push down on your outside pedal.

✗ Don't allow your inside pedal to drift downwards.

✓ Push your inside hand slightly forward to create the turn.

✗ Don't force the movement on the handlebars.

✓ Choose your line as you approach the corner.

✗ Don't allow your weight to be shifted forward.

Downhill

1 Build your confidence slowly when increasing your downhill speed.

2 Keep your hands on the drops during the descent so you are more able to react if there is a problem ahead.

3 Adopt a streamlined position to reduce wind resistance.

There are two types of downhill riding you need to master: straight and cornering. You need a good technique in the first instance but after that it is a matter of being stronger than your fear. But that does not mean taking undue risks.

Build your confidence and your speed slowly as you learn to trust the techniques for going downhill at speed. The fastest downhill professional cyclists push themselves to the very edge, using every millimetre of the road to maximize their speed. It is not necessary to take your downhill racing to such extremes but learning how to race effectively at speed will be an important part of improving your times and your position in your races.

When cycling downhill in a straight line or a very gradual bend you can adopt a more streamlined position to reduce wind resistance and increase your speed. This requires you to lower your back, shoulders and head into a more horizontal position. This will cause your back to stretch out and may require you to slide back in your seat slightly.

You may have seen some professional cyclists descending with their hands almost together, centred on the top of the handlebars to minimize the wind resistance. This is something only advanced cyclists attempt (and then, not even all of them). The time-saving advantage is minimal and reduces your ability to react if there is a problem on the road ahead such as a stone or a hole.

Keep your hands on your drops so your hands are close to the shifters. Certainly do not attempt to copy the crazy downhillers who descend with their stomach balanced on the saddle and their eyes peering just over the handlebars as if they are riding a rocket!

When cornering downhill at speed you will almost automatically need to use the counter-steering method (see pages 50-51). The key point is to always focus on keeping your body weight driving through the centre of the bicycle.

This is important because on a downhill your body weight will be naturally pitched forwards unless you concentrate on keeping it back and centred. On extreme downhills you may have seen professionals shifting backwards in their saddle as they approach a corner, which is them ensuring their weight is centred (as well as a way of increasing braking efficiency). Remember, the steepness of the downhill and the resulting speed you enter into a corner determines how much you will be pitched forward and therefore how much adjustment you will need to make.

You should be aware that if you go too far back your rear tyre might start to slip. Gradually, with experience, you will learn to feel the right amount of adjustment needed to stay centred.

Braking into a corner, because of the pressure applied to the front wheel, will also cause your body to be pitched forward, so concentrate on applying even pressure to both brakes. Too much pressure on the front brake increases the chance of sliding, especially during the wet weather.

Before taking a sharp corner apply your brakes early enough to ensure you enter the corner at a speed that allows you to take that corner without braking again. Because you are leaning into the bend your tyres' contact with the road is reduced and therefore braking at this time is more likely to cause you to slide away. Again, slowly build your confidence as you gradually learn the correct

speed at which to enter a corner without the need to brake as you take it.

Remember, although it is unlikely that any two corners in the world are exactly the same, the more corners you take successfully and the faster you are able to take them at, the more you will build your confidence. Downhill speed and downhill cornering is a matter of trial and error – try to use trial and not error because error can be a very painful experience when you are

travelling on two wheels at 50 kph (31 mph).

Finally, consider that in hilly and mountainous environments you will frequently encounter lower temperatures. Practice putting on a wind jacket as you are cycling and get into the habit of putting it on as you are about to enter the descent. Over time you can become quite proficient at putting on your jacket quickly (and taking it off when you have completed your descent). Obviously you can skip this if the temperatures are soaring!

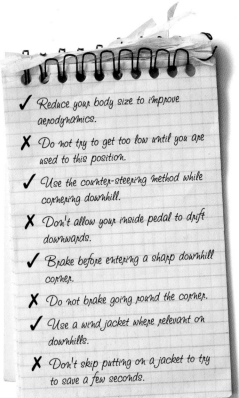

✓ Reduce your body size to improve aerodynamics.

✗ Do not try to get too low until you are used to this position.

✓ Use the counter-steering method while cornering downhill.

✗ Don't allow your inside pedal to drift downwards.

✓ Brake before entering a sharp downhill corner.

✗ Do not brake going round the corner.

✓ Use a wind jacket where relevant on downhills.

✗ Don't skip putting on a jacket to try to save a few seconds.

4 Concentrate on keeping centred over your bicycle as entering a bend downhill will naturally pitch you forward.

5 Apply your brakes before entering a sharp bend not during the turn.

6 Apply both brakes evenly when cycling downhill as too much pressure on the front increases the chance of sliding.

Rain & wet weather

1 Always carry a rain jacket even if the weather looks fine when you leave home.

2 Don't forget your hands, head and legs – wear gloves, helmet and apply leg cream.

3 Wear bright colours for visibility as motor vehicles have impaired vision in the wet weather.

Cycling in rainy weather and getting soaking wet is certainly not a pleasant experience. Even in summer, when it's relatively warm, riding in the rain can cause your body temperature to drop. When you avoid taking appropriate steps to stay warm you will feel weaker and your performance will inevitably decrease quite significantly.

When your body starts to get cold, one of its first defence mechanisms is to shunt blood flow to the torso and away from the extremities. Depending on the season and where you live you will have to accept that you can't always avoid an uncomfortable 'cold shower'.

Unless you're going out for a bike ride on a hot summer day you should always carry a lightweight waterproof jacket in the pocket of your jersey. Even if it looks fine when you leave your house, still take your jacket because, as we all know, weather conditions can quickly change and when you are wet and cold the trip back home will be very unpleasant. However, if you wear the right gear a wet day can turn out to be a challenge that even the most fair-weather riders will undergo with a smile.

Rain jackets are probably the most important component of surviving

a rainy day on the bike. Note that some of these lightweight cycling jackets are not completely waterproof. In a heavy downpour, water will start to be absorbed by the fabric and if your jacket doesn't have a waterproof layer under it, water will begin to seep through.

The simplest form of a rain jacket is made of clear plastic. These are highly effective for keeping you warm because they are 100 per cent waterproof. However, they don't breathe well at all. As soon as you start exercising you will get damp inside the jacket from the moisture your body produces. As you work harder your body tends to increase the amount it sweats and you may actually be less damp without

the jacket than when wearing it! This type of jacket is therefore only suitable for short-term non-strenuous use, for example in descents when you don't have to push hard on your pedals.

Modern breathable rain jackets offer the best choice for cycling in the rain. They are first of all waterproof and windproof and secondly they attempt to allow moisture from inside to escape through the breathable fabric without letting water come in the other way. You therefore get something that breathes combined with pretty good rain resistance, even during long periods of wet weather. When it is raining it often becomes quite dark, especially in winter months.

Drivers will have problems to see cyclists, as the rain reduces their visibility, so preferably wear a rain jacket with a highly visible colour.

When your body starts to get cold one of its first defence mechanisms is to shunt blood flow to the torso and away from the extremities (head, feet and hands). So as well as putting on your rain jacket you should also pay attention to keeping your head, feet and hands warm.

Waterproof overshoes are a must when the weather is wet and cool. They fit closely over your cycling shoes with a Velcro fastening strip or a zipper at the back. As well as keeping your feet warm and dry, overshoes also have the added side effect of keeping your shoes clean.

Then you have to think about your hands. While you are riding your hands are relatively inactive and therefore getting cold during chilly, rainy weather. Winter gloves, consisting of a waterproof exterior layer and another layer of insulation are therefore vital for protecting your hands from cold, wind and rain.

Glasses are another important element of your cycling gear. They prevent insects from getting into your eyes in the summer and during rainy weather they help to avoid water and sand from wet roads spraying into your eyes. This is something that especially happens when you are riding in a group.

Last but not least, never go out for a ride without wearing a helmet. During wet days also wear a winter cap under your helmet as well to keep your head warm.

When you expect it's going to be cool and rainy, start the day with a layer of warming cream on your legs. This cream has a waterproof action, providing a warming sensation as well as stimulating a rapid blood supply to muscle tissues to allow better oxygenation and therefore reducing the risk of accumulating lactic acid. After applying a warming cream you can apply a layer of Vaseline as well for even more protection.

Consider the following points when cycling in wet weather:

- Avoid staying too close to the gutter because glass and stones usually build up there.
- Reduce the pressure of your tyres to around 100 psi (or seven bar) to allow a larger contact patch at the tyre-to-pavement contact point.
- Reduce your speed before cornering. When brakes become wet, stopping time increases a lot. Practice braking to get used to the effects of the water. Pump your brakes gently while going downhill to reduce your bicycle's speed slightly and dry the rims a bit.
- Be careful when riding on the painted stripes of zebra crossings, leaves and manhole covers, as they become slippery in the wet. Avoid turning sharply on these surfaces.
- Look out for trails of mud and animal dung on country roads.
- Remember that motor vehicles have less control and visibility in wet weather.

✓ Always carry a rain jacket.

✗ Don't think because the weather looks fine you shouldn't carry one.

✓ Accept that you will have to ride slower in wet weather.

✗ Don't get frustrated at your slower times – wet weather is a reality.

✓ Keep your eyes open for zebra crossings, leaves and manhole covers which are slippery in the wet.

✗ Avoid turning sharply on these surfaces.

✓ Gently pump your brakes when going downhill.

✗ Accept that your braking will be impaired in the wet.

4 Reduce your tyre pressure for greater grip on the road.

5 Reduce your speed when cornering in the wet. Don't try to maintain your dry weather speeds.

6 Pump your brakes gently when going downhill to reduce speed and help dry off your rims.

Windy weather

1 In a side wind stay diagonally behind the rider in front of you on the side away from the wind.

2 The more the wind blows the more you need to move forward next to the rider shielding you.

3 The more you are back in the line the more you will benefit from wind resistance.

There are three types of wind – headwind, tailwind and side wind. Each affects your riding style and you constantly need to think about the wind direction. A strong headwind is seen by many cyclists as one of their biggest enemies. However, it is a fact of cycling and you have to deal with it and adapt your drafting technique (see pages 42-45) accordingly.

Ask professional cyclists their most feared natural barrier and they will mention the 'horrible' crosswind. Wind from the side makes a good drafting technique even more important because if you are not able to stay away from the side wind by drafting another rider you are inevitably going to be dropped from the peloton. Maybe you remember some stages of the Tour de France where on a flat section of the course the peloton splits into several smaller groups and rides as a cohesive unit in a diagonal shape (or what is known as a echelon)?

Echelon formation occurs when cyclists are exposed to side wind. This drafting technique allows cyclists to secure a proper position in the peloton when their competitors are trying to use the crosswinds to split up the group. To stay protected from the wind and get the advantage of drafting you should stay diagonally behind the rider in front of you on the side away from the wind. This means if the wind is blowing from the left, you have to ride on the right side of the person in front of you.

The more the wind blows the more you have to move forward next to him on the leeward side to reduce wind resistance. Obviously, the rider leading the group is most exposed to the wind. The next rider staying diagonally behind the first rider on the leeward side has less wind resistance and each next rider down the line will be rewarded with an even greater benefit.

However, the first rider, setting the pace, will not be able to maintain this position for a long as he needs time to recover. Hence he will pull off, slow down and allow the second rider to take over the lead position, while starting to move diagonally backwards behind the other riders until reaching the other side of the road. The group will be divided into a group of riders creating a leading line and a group creating a recovery line, rotating in a way that every rider alternately gets the chance to pull at the front and to recover.

This means that if the wind is coming from the right, the entire leading line of riders shift to the right, moving diagonally forward to the windward side of the road while leaving a space on the leeward side of the road for the rider who just left his leading position and is now moving diagonally backwards behind the leading line until it's his turn to move forward again. The total number of riders that can rotate through an echelon will depend on the width of the road. A wide road will give space to 15 or more riders, a narrow road can result in an echelon of sometimes not more than four to five riders.

✓ In a side wind always ride in a echelon formation to conserve energy.

✗ Don't try to fight the wind alone.

✓ The more the wind blows the more you need to move forward to be closer to the rider next to you.

✗ If you leave a gap you will not benefit.

✓ When the rider in front pulls off after his stint move across to allow him space to move to the back of the echelon.

✗ Don't try to skip your turn at the front.

✓ After your turn at the front, drop off and slowly make your way to the back.

✗ Don't fear the wind – it is a part of your cycling experience.

fitness & training

// FASTER // FITTER // MORE MOTIVATED

The basics

Cycling is a fantastic way to improve your fitness, lose weight, relieve stress and strengthen your cardiovascular system. An effective training programme starts with having a clear vision of your own objectives and should be designed in line with your experience level, schedule and personal lifestyle. All these aspects must be taken into account to help you feel at ease with your own programme.

You've probably wondered how your muscles produce the energy needed to power your bicycle. The answer might appear simple: breathe in oxygen, your lungs will send this to your muscles where the fuels from various nutritional elements combine with the oxygen and your muscles contract to produce force. Do this for a period of time and you'll become stronger and faster. Yes, this sounds okay, but what actually happened?

To assure the transport of chemical energy within the cells of your muscle fibres, your body produces a molecular fuel, called ATP (adenosine triphosphate) from the food you eat. Muscles cannot contract without ATP and nearly all the metabolic functions in your body depend on it. Your body produces ATP in two different ways during exercise – aerobically (with air) and anaerobically (without air). The anaerobic system is divided again into two different systems: the immediate anaerobic energy system and the short-term anaerobic energy system (or the so-called adenosine triphosphate (ATP)/creatine phosphate (CP) System).

Oxygen is necessary for most of your body's ATP needs. When you are riding easily and have enough oxygen to chat with your friend, the greatest part of your ATP for muscular work is produced aerobically. But when you increase your intensity it becomes more difficult to control your breathing and harder to continue the conversation. Your body will be obliged to change the way it produces energy and your anaerobic energy system takes over.

During high-intensity exercise your muscles have the capacity to produce energy when the cardiovascular system is unable to deliver sufficient oxygen to the muscles to meet your energy needs. It will do this with less oxygen and the energy will be produced anaerobically. The anaerobic system allows you to attain high speeds, but the waste product building up in your muscles, called lactic acid, causes a burning sensation and forces you to slow down. The aerobic system in cycling is the most important one because it produces most of the energy needed to sustain daily training sessions.

This is the most important system endurance cyclists need to train in order to save the anaerobic and ATP/CP energy systems for when they are needed. This requires high volumes of slow- and medium-intensity riding. Training times depend on the length of the race being targeted but in general three to four hours of basic endurance sessions at slow, medium and some anaerobic threshold intensity are sufficient to improve this system.

Although carbohydrate is your body's preferred source of fuel during activity, fat also supplies energy. Aerobic training increases your body's ability to mobilize fat as an energy source at intensities below the anaerobic threshold – your body learns to be more 'fat efficient'. This will improve your capacity to sustain long distances. The optimal intensity to improve your fat-burning capability is about 80 per cent of maximum heart rate.

The aerobic system has these characteristics:
1. It provides fuel (glucose) to the cells through the synthesis of glycogen, carbohydrate, fat, and protein.

2. Synthesis takes place within the presence of oxygen, with the only by-products being CO_2 and water.

3. Limited production of lactic acid with maximum blood lactate levels of four mmol/L.

4. Energy production can continue indefinitely provided your body is well hydrated and fed and workloads remain low enough that the aerobic system remains the primary energy provider.

The immediate anaerobic energy system (ATP/CP)

When your body generates energy through the ATP/CP system, no oxygen is needed to produce energy and it supplies energy for a maximum of six to eight seconds. One of the situations where this might be used is sprinting. Sprinters need explosiveness and have to optimize this energy system. Too much aerobic training can undermine this explosiveness as it can reduce the peak-power capability of our power and speed-generating fast-twitch muscle fibres.

The ATP/CP system has these characteristics:

1. The system has the ability to provide a brief but intense amount of energy for the times when the body must do a large amount of work over a brief period time.

2. Glycolysis (the metabolic breakdown of glucose and other sugars without oxygen) is not involved so the process is not catabolic.

3. The system can, and should be trained, by doing short maximum intervals with comparatively long recovery times to replenish the ATP/CP stores.

4. Rebuilding of the supply of ATP takes 24 to 48 hours.

The short-term anaerobic energy system

Like its immediate energy system brother, the short-term anaerobic energy system also produces high-powered energy. However, it is more enduring and can provide energy for up to 90 seconds. Once the aerobic system can no longer supply sufficient oxygen to the cells the process of converting glycogen to glucose and then to ATP shortens but there is an expensive price to pay for this.

Glycogen resources are used up rapidly and the body significantly increases the production of lactic acid. Nevertheless, the system can be trained and this strengthens the muscles' ability to adapt to this process and absorb lactic acid more efficiently. Doing interval workouts above your anaerobic threshold will fine-tune this system. By doing these high-intensity sessions the stimulus to your body is sufficient to incite improved lactate tolerance. But don't overdo it as extended work above the anaerobic threshold triggers catabolic waste and damages muscle cells.

The anaerobic energy system has these characteristics:

1. It is capable of supplying fuel to the cells when there is an oxygen deficit.

2. It allows well-trained cyclists to maintain high workloads for about an hour to an hour and a half.

3. It can respond to high workloads quicker than the aerobic system and therefore cyclists focusing on endurance-based disciplines won't have to spend a large amount of training time to improve this energy system.

4. Due to the lack of oxygen, glycolysis takes place and this is catabolic (destructive) to the muscle cells if the process continues for too long. Excessive anaerobic training undermines the aerobic energy system.

5. Fuel resources are used up rapidly and the body cannot synthesize fats and protein quick enough to supply this system so glycogen and carbohydrates must be used.

Anaerobic threshold

Anaerobic threshold is the exercise intensity at which lactic acid starts to accumulate in your bloodstream. Riding at or just below the anaerobic threshold allows you to maintain your rhythm during a long climb, a breakaway or a time trial.

This intensity is often referred to as the point of 'pushing hard' as you are riding in the threshold between when the ATP for muscular contraction is coming mainly from aerobic metabolism and when anaerobic metabolism starts to contribute at a high rate.

Once you pass the anaerobic threshold, superfluous lactic acid produced by your muscles starts to accumulate. Generally this occurs when riding at an intensity of between 80 per cent and 90 per cent of maximum heart rate or between 80 and 90 per cent of power at the anaerobic threshold when expressed in watts.

Training sessions in this zone allow you to increase the speed or effort you can maintain before lactic acid causes the burning pain in your muscles and you slow down. If the pace you hold at your lactate threshold is higher than the pace your competitor holds at his anaerobic threshold, you go faster, reach the finish first, and win.

Lactate threshold Test

Lactate threshold (LT) testing can be utilized to determine the correct training intensity and monitor your progression. This method includes blood taken from the finger or ear to determine the amount of lactate.

There are numerous protocols – this is an example of one used by several famous sport physiologists. First, warm up for about 20 minutes on the indoor trainer or ergometer at an easy load. After the first four-minute stage, increase workload by 30 watts every four minutes and in the last minute of each stage record heart rate and blood lactate.

Cyclists are typically able to pass six to nine stages before reaching maximum effort. Sometimes the test is broken off when a break point in the blood lactate values has been distinguished. This break point area is known as the lactate threshold, or anaerobic threshold. You are said to have crossed the anaerobic threshold when lactate concentration increases by one mmol/L or more in the succeeding stages. By repeating these tests you can monitor aspects of your condition such as increased power and/or speed at the anaerobic threshold, improved efficiency of the metabolic system and a higher power- (or speed-) to-weight ratio.

Conconi Test

The Conconi Test will also measure the approximate values of your maximum and anaerobic threshold rates. The test records your heart rate at regular intervals while workloads are progressively increasing. The heart rate increases (approximately) linearly up to the deflection point, where the heart rate reaches the anaerobic threshold. The points are plotted on a graph with heart rate on one axis and load (or speed) on the other with the graph's deflection point indicating the anaerobic threshold.

Field test

If you do not have access to a testing centre use a simple field test. You need a heart-rate monitor and a five to 10 kilometre (three to six mile) section of road that is either flat or uphill (a six to eight per cent grade). Warm up properly before starting. Perform the ride at the fastest pace you can sustain at a steady effort with no loss of speed.

During this effort record your average and maximum heart rate (and wattage if you have a power meter). Generally cyclists average about five to seven per cent above anaerobic power threshold and anaerobic heart-rate threshold levels for such a distance during a field test.

Resistance training

Cycling is in the first instance an endurance sport with the major energy contribution coming from aerobic energy production. But strength and power also play a significant role. It's important to remember that resistance training (also called strength training) is primarily an anaerobic activity characterized by short bursts of intense activity.

As a road cyclist you will often need to climb short, steep hills, react to accelerations in speed and sprint at the end of a race. In these cases you will need strength and power and have to produce energy anaerobically. Therefore, resistance training plays an important role in almost every training programme. Studies on exercise physiology have shown an extended period of strength training with free weights and/ or machines leads to significantly increased leg strength and reduced fatigue levels during cycling.

While leg strength increases, oxygen consumption at a given power level appears not to increase, which is a sign of improved aerobic capacity. There are also indications that increased strength reduces the risk of injuries. Resistance training is an important part of a post-injury rehabilitation. So both endurance and resistance training are needed

to improve performance. The time you spend on your bicycle remains the most important element of your training programme. But varying amounts of time and intensity, both on the bicycle and in the gym, need to be part of your overall training programme.

Planning your resistance programme

Resistance training must be viewed as a supplemental training element to riding – a means to a better end. A resistance-training programme for a cyclist must be specific, dynamic, organized and adaptable. Everything starts with proper planning and therefore the concept of periodization should be used when defining an appropriate yearly training programme. The gradual build-up of your resistance-training programme should match with the mesocycles of the periodization for your training programme (see Training programmes on pages 138-159).

Resistance training in the gym

Before any workout in the gym you should warm up for around 15-20 minutes in your Level 1 zone (see Training programmes on page 146) on a stationary bicycle or ergometer. Between sets of lower body exercises you should ride for five to 10 minutes to help maintain

your agility and smooth pedalling style. Finish every training session with a cool down of 10 minutes – heart rates during serious strength training fluctuate with Level 2 intensity (see Training programmes on page 146). Additional stretching is welcome as well, both before and after resistance workouts. And always wear proper shoes with firm soles designed to prevent instability.

One repetition maximum

The weight you use to execute an exercise is expressed as a percentage of the maximum amount of weight you are able to lift in a single repetition for a given exercise and is called the 'one repetition maximum' (or 1RM). This test should be performed with a qualified strength coach for reasons of safety.

Transitional phase

The start of your resistance programme takes place at the beginning of the transitional phase and focuses on preparing your muscles to the stimulus of resistance training. Exercises should be done at a low intensity with little equipment as you mainly use your body weight to avoid muscle stress by using too much weight too early.

Foundation phase

During the foundation phase, when

the total volume of endurance work is relatively low, resistance training should be emphasized more than during other training periods and you should spend three days per week in the gym. The aim is to generate muscle hypertrophy (the increase in the volume of muscle tissue due to the enlargement of its muscle cells). You should increase loads to reach a moderate intensity while decreasing the number of repetitions. By allowing the muscles to work more intensively they 'grow' (hypertrophy) and properly prepare for the next period.

Preparation phase/basic strength

During the basic strength period you aim to increase the strength of individual muscle groups by doing specific exercises. Loads are increased to the maximum while the number of repetitions decreases. The exercises are focused mainly on combined (supporting) muscle groups and you should pay special attention to your weakest muscle groups.

Specialization phase/power phase

As the name indicates, this phase is about the power you can develop on your bicycle. More power will allow you, for example, to jump more quickly, react to changes in rhythm easier and to chase down breakaways at a higher pace. During the power phase you have to reduce the load but concentrate on doing the exercises explosively.

Competition phase/muscular endurance

This is the peaking phase of your season. In the first month of this period continue with resistance training twice a week. Focus on building muscular endurance by increasing the number of repetitions per exercise in combination with special strength training on the bicycle.

As a general rule you have to stop weight training at least two weeks before your goal event because it takes about two to three weeks for your legs to completely adapt their muscle memory to the movement speed inherent with the pedal stroke and to lose the muscle memory of the slower cadence of lifting weights. After your peak period you can gradually pick up some resistance training again to maintain strength levels, although the emphasis should be on racing and building endurance and tempo.

This will improve your leg speed significantly and you will not lose the gains you made up to this point. You can continue upper body exercises until the week of your event but cease core work the week before to give your body every ounce of its energy for the event.

Strength hill intervals

Strength hill interval training is resistance training on the bicycle to increase the strength of specific muscles involved in your pedal stroke. Basically you have to ride uphill with a low cadence of around 50 RPM while focusing on a nice circular pedal stroke. This training allows you to increase the force peak for each pedal stroke.

If you don't have an opportunity to ride uphill, the ergometer or indoor cycling trainer is an alternative. Both explosive power and muscular endurance can be improved significantly. Muscular endurance intervals should be performed at a cadence of 50-60 RPM at an endurance and tempo intensity. You should feel a gentle burn and fatigue in your leg muscles, but not the oxygen-debt, lactic-acid burn that you would get from a maximum effort hill climb. You should never exceed your anaerobic threshold – think 'weight room on the bicycle'.

Training for speed and power

Once you have addressed some solid base training you can start to train on your sprints. Make sure you look at how the races you are preparing for finish and tailor your sprint work to that. Depending on the time of year and your goals for the season, sprints can be worked on throughout the season. As you move towards your goal event reduce the frequency and intensity of speed training.

Hill sprints

On a short hill of about a five per cent to 10 per cent grade do a session of uphill sprints, going all-out to the top for 15 seconds. This will develop your anaerobic power and peak force but you expose your muscles and ligaments to significant stress, so before you start with this exercise warm up for at least half an hour.

Start the exercise riding very slowly and jump, almost from a standstill, in an all-out sprint while staying seated, to the top. Novice and young cyclists should avoid using gears that are too big – opt for the relatively small gear of 42-16-15. More experienced cyclists should choose a bigger gear to get the maximum results. A world-renowned cyclist like Davide Rebellin, for example, uses a 53-15 on a 13-14 per cent grade.

After each uphill sprint recover for two minutes using a light gear to release muscle tension. During the foundation period, start slowly by limiting the total number of repetitions per training to a maximum of five or six. Then gradually increase to 15-18 repetitions at the end of the preparation period.

Flat sprints

Start at a speed of about 20 kph (12 mph) in your big ring and the smaller cogs on the rear cassette. Then stand up and explode on the pedals. Don't shift, muscle the bicycle up to speed by accelerating against the resistance. Hold this effort for 15-20 seconds. Take at least five minutes to make sure you completely recover between each burst. Complete three to 12 of these sprints per ride, twice a week, over the course of two to three weeks.

Ins and outs

Once you have worked on the strength for sprints move to more traditional sprint workouts by getting in and out of the saddle. These workouts strive to simulate what you may experience in the final kilometres of a race and are best done with the wind at your back. Start with a short burst of acceleration out of the saddle in a big gear when riding at about 30 kph (19 mph), then sit back in

your saddle for a short period where the sprint effort levels off slightly. Then launch your final surge out of the saddle again – give it everything! Each time you get up and sit back maintain the position for about five to seven seconds. Work up to three to five sprints like this, each about 15-20 seconds long with a recovery of five minutes between each sprint. This drill improves your ability to accelerate several times during a longer sprint.

Downhill sprints

When on a descent, start sprinting for 20 seconds (on a straight road) forcing your legs to spin as fast as they can while you stay seated. Execute these sprints during a long bicycle ride – five to six repetitions are sufficient. This exercise allows you to improve the inter-muscular coordination of all muscles involved in the pedal stroke, especially between the quads and hamstrings.

A good coordination results in reduced energy expenditure and greater pedal efficiency and ultimately leads to increased power output. This is one of the best ways to simulate high-speed sprint finishes when you don't have the benefit of a lead out or charging field of riders. This is very beneficial the day after a workout in the gym, because you recover your agility.

Over-training and over-reaching

The sensation of fatigue is necessary because it lets you know you are pushing your physical limits. You train to improve your performance and your body generally reacts positively to being 'pushed'. However, in certain circumstances, if your body is over-stimulated or stimulated incorrectly, you will suffer adverse effects.

Levels of fatigue

1. The first level of fatigue is 'bonking', which is hypoglycemia – the term for abnormally low levels of blood glucose. You bonk when you have exhausted your glycogen stores, haven't ingested enough carbohydrates to produce more blood glucose, and are still cycling.

2. Post-ride fatigue is a natural response to several hours of intense exercise, which tells you that you are pushing your normal training limits.

3. Over-reaching is the next step up and is when short-term performance drops and develops as a result of intense training sessions during a 'high-load' microcycle. Symptoms are those of normal fatigue. The right amount of recovery will allow you to become faster and stronger. It is, however, a warning.

4. Over-training is the debilitating and long-term (often lasting weeks and sometimes months) fatigue, which degrades rather than stimulates performance.

How to prevent over-training

Cyclists seem to be one of the few groups capable of reaching the over-trained level of fatigue. And it isn't necessary to undertake an extensive training programme to be at risk. In fact, often novice cyclists, working out periodically with relatively light training schedules, can also suffer. While a professional cyclist might consider an 80-kilometre (50-mile) ride part of a light recovery week, your 30-kilometre (19-mile) ride could produce all the symptoms of overtraining if you don't adapt certain aspects of your lifestyle.

The most frequent causes of over-training are: excessive increase in training loads, insufficient recovery periods, poor diet (insufficient quantity of carbohydrates or other nutritional elements), travel factors and a lack of training variety.

So how do you prevent over-training? You need the balance between training and recovery both at long term (macrocycle/mesocycle) and short term (microcycle) (see page 143). In endurance sports the maximum recommended 'load-period' during a mesocycle (of high intensity/volume) is about three weeks. After this load-period, training intensity should be reduced in the fourth week and the number of rest days increased. The purpose of this recovery week is to allow your body complete regeneration. Most training programmes include one or two rest days per week as well as a day or two of easy spinning, allowing you to recover.

Over-reaching is a normal part of the training cycle but a few days of recovery should be sufficient to notice an improvement in your performance. If you still feel tired after a few days it could be a sign that you have trained too much at a high intensity (stimulating your anaerobic system) which means it's time to switch to more aerobic training, keeping you at 70 per cent of your maximum heart rate.

Continuing anaerobic sessions could lead to entering the zone of overtraining which will put you out for several weeks. Unvaried training programmes, or programmes without alternating periods of high and low volume/intensity, also severely increase the risk of over-training. The key is planning your own personal training programme to occasionally over-reach but not over-train. Your challenge is finding your own individual boundary.

Stretches

Stretching plays a crucial role in injury prevention and enhancing overall athletic performance and yet it is often overlooked and neglected by many athletes as the 'soft' part of the training programme. Stretching is every bit as important as pushing a big, heavy weight or putting in those extra high-intensity kilometres in your training. Don't miss your stretching regime just to get in a few more minutes hard training. It's the wrong move.

By training regularly you will be shortening certain muscles. To ensure you maintain an equal muscular balance throughout your body it is imperative you do not skip the stretches that help to keep these muscles in shape. Although it is important to stretch before a session to prepare for what is to follow, it is also vital to stretch afterwards as well.

This can be hard to do after a tough session or race but generally athletes should spend a lot longer stretching after a heavy training session than before it. In general, it is best to do your stretching at the end of a workout, stretching out the muscles you have just worked for a minimum of one minute each. This will help prevent the shortening of muscles and muscular imbalances in your body, which can cause pain,

injury and may also stop you from training or competing.

So, for example, if you have performed a set of squats you will need to stretch your quads, hamstrings, glutes, calves and lower back. This is just basic maintenance stretching. When you start to clock up more kilometres in training it is advisable to use your rest days to take deeper and longer stretches. Many people neglect this area of their training. A day off is a day off a lot of us think. But get into the habit of giving those muscles you have worked so hard during the week, a really good stretch. You can also do your maintenance stretches on your rest breaks when training.

For the deeper stretches, which really improve your flexibility and balance, it's advisable to find a suitable yoga or stretch class. Stretching really can make a difference between achieving your goals and failing to get to the start line. Take it seriously, do not think it's just something you need to get out of the way before the serious work: this is part of the serious work.

Consider also that before a training session or important race your stress levels can rise, so before stretching you should consider

paying attention to what most of us take for granted: breathing. Slowly take a couple of long breaths in and out through your nose. Or take one big, deep breath from your stomach. In sport, especially at the highest level, small details can make a significant difference. That's why even a tiny relief from your stress might result in finding just that energy you need even if it's just for a few seconds to help keep you focused and relaxed.

Over the next few pages you will see details of some key stretches. You can use these before and after training/racing but do not neglect to do these stretches on your day off. Also, while these are key stretches for many of the muscles you will use, do not rely on these entirely. Remember to stretch out as many muscles as possible to keep muscular balance.

Stretches – seated back twist

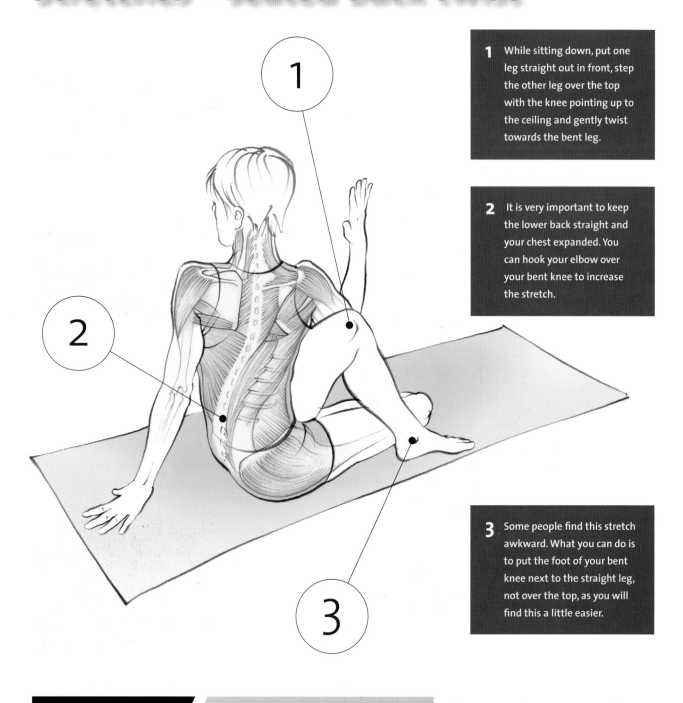

1 While sitting down, put one leg straight out in front, step the other leg over the top with the knee pointing up to the ceiling and gently twist towards the bent leg.

2 It is very important to keep the lower back straight and your chest expanded. You can hook your elbow over your bent knee to increase the stretch.

3 Some people find this stretch awkward. What you can do is to put the foot of your bent knee next to the straight leg, not over the top, as you will find this a little easier.

MUSCLES STRETCHED BACK, SHOULDERS AND BACK

Stretches – forward bend

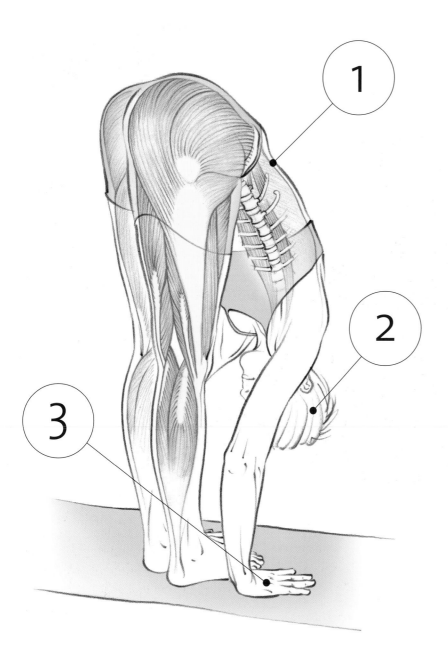

1 Start by standing tall with your feet slightly apart, tuck your chin into your chest and roll down as far as you can. Don't worry if your hand doesn't touch the floor.

2 Keep looking through your knees behind you and allow the weight of your head to pull you down. Don't force the stretch.

3 If your hands can touch the floor, try pressing the palm of your hands into the ground. If the stretch is too uncomfortable keep your knees soft.

MUSCLES STRETCHED   *BACK, GLUTES, HAMSTRINGS & CALVES*

Stretches – calf

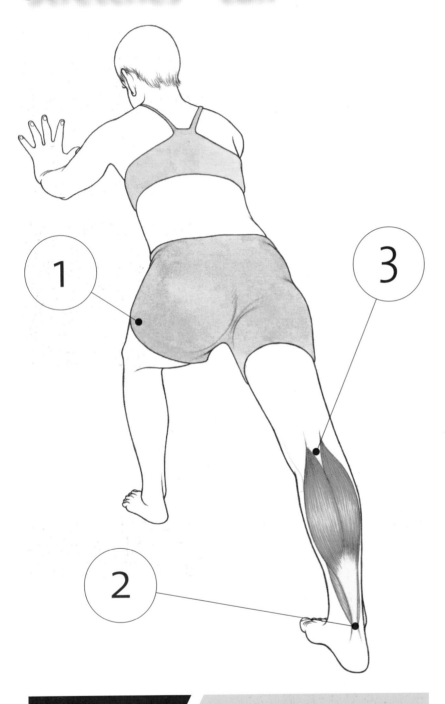

1 With your hands leaning against a wall, step one leg back keeping the leg straight and bending your front leg. Work the back heel into the floor.

2 To keep the stretch true make sure your weight is pressing forward and your back heel is lengthening.

3 To work the shorter muscle of the calf you can simply bend the back knee while still working the back heel down to the floor.

MUSCLES STRETCHED   *CALVES*

Stretches – seated adductor

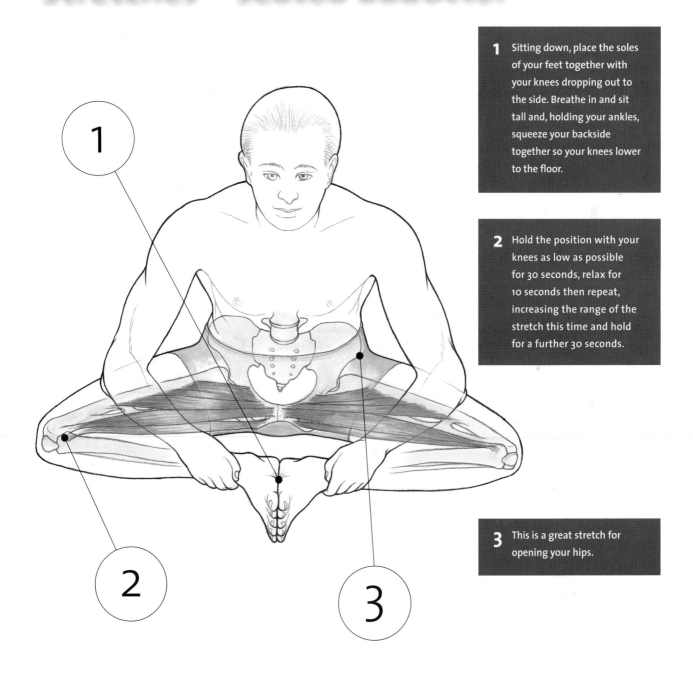

1. Sitting down, place the soles of your feet together with your knees dropping out to the side. Breathe in and sit tall and, holding your ankles, squeeze your backside together so your knees lower to the floor.

2. Hold the position with your knees as low as possible for 30 seconds, relax for 10 seconds then repeat, increasing the range of the stretch this time and hold for a further 30 seconds.

3. This is a great stretch for opening your hips.

MUSCLES STRETCHED   *ADDUCTORS*

cross training

// STRONGER // TOUGHER
// MORE POWERFUL

The basics

If you are training for a particular sport there is no question that the best way to get fit for that purpose is to actually do that sport. If you want to be a cyclist then cycle, cycle and cycle some more, it's as simple as that.

So why cross train then?

Here we focus on four reasons to cross train: strengthening a weakness in a particular muscle or muscle group, injury prevention, motivation and ensuring that you maintain your general fitness.

Most coaches will include a strength-training programme into an athlete's schedule whatever sport they are involved in. The amount of work that needs to be done in the gym can vary from sport to sport and, of course, the distance you are training for and the specific goals you have.

Generally, the shorter events will require more power and strength, which can be gained with weights. For endurance events it is advisable that the strength training is done well away from the heavy road work. For example, if you are considering entering an event in six months, start your gym work with heavy weights and low reps (eight to 12 reps) for six to eight weeks, then lower the weights but increase the reps (maximum 15) for a couple of weeks. After this you can then start to eliminate all weight work and concentrate on your cycling.

However, everything depends on how serious and challenging your targets are. You can keep working on the strength training after these guidelines but be aware that your cycling could suffer as muscle fatigue may prevent you training properly for your main event. If you don't want to give up your cross training completely you could substitute this gym work for increased core work or specific stretching exercises. Overall, then, the benefits of spending time in the gym will be extra power on the road, but don't overdo it – your training should always keep your core goals in mind.

Identify and strengthen weaknesses in the chain

One benefit of cross training is targeting a particular weakness in your body that is holding your cycling back. Once you have identified that weakness in your body while cycling you can head to the gym and really focus on that particular area, whether it's your legs, your shoulders or simply building up muscle groups for general body balance. So, for example, if you find some weakness in your hamstrings (back of the leg) and glutes (backside) while cycling you can use the squats (see page 90) and hamstring curls (see page 92) to strengthen these areas. By focussing on these muscles in the gym you really will notice a difference when you are cycling.

However, it must still be remembered at all times that a lot of the pain we experience is due to the build up of lactic acid and the best way to combat this is to train in your chosen sport to keep the essential muscles for cycling in active use.

Injury prevention

Prevention of injury is probably the main reason to do specific training for your sport. Injuries can ruin months of hard work and for us non-sporting professionals, as well as ruining the sporting dream, this can make daily life very uncomfortable – just ask anyone with bad back pain they picked up in sport who has to sit in an office for eight hours a day.

When increasing your training workload on the road you may experience discomfort in your body, as muscles are asked to perform tasks at a much higher level to anything they have known before. For example, if your hamstrings

become very strong and tight and your opposite muscles (the quads) are weak then this can cause the pelvis to be held in a tilted alignment, which in turn causes poor back alignment and back pain.

For these reasons, in the strength programmes outlined (see pages 109-111) you will find exercises which are not only geared towards cycling, but will also help keep a good muscular balance in your body. In the core section you will also find some Pilates exercises.

These exercises are slightly modified for ease of use. However, if you can attend some Pilates or yoga classes these are an excellent way of keeping your core strong, maintaining an equal muscle balance and keeping your muscles supple. The added benefit of these exercises is that as these exercises are low impact there is a reduced risk of injury and because of the

low-energy output they can even be done on your rest day.

Stretching regularly also plays a key role in injury prevention and this aspect of your training should not be ignored (See Fitness & training pages 78-83).

Motivation
Sometimes, when training for a specific event, you will just need a break from the routine of pounding the road. By having one day a week where you train your body in a different way you can really freshen up your mind as well. It can also be a good idea to add in some basic targets for your resistance training to keep motivated. You could, for instance, aim to increase your weight load by a certain percentage over a two-month period.

Be aware that the targets you set will very much depend on where

your starting point is. If you are already experienced in strength training your gains will be small because you will already have reached a decent level, so be realistic when setting goals.

General fitness
Many people start on their cycling journey as a way of getting into shape and this is one of the greatest benefits of the sport. However, you must remember that if you just train in the sport you will only be fit for this sport. A certain amount of fitness will cross over to other fitness areas, but to keep yourself healthy and looking good often requires something a bit more specific. This can be seen clearly in different running distances. A good 100-metre runner will often struggle to do a good marathon time and vice-versa. So if one of your goals from cycling is good overall health you should not ignore cross training.

Legs – squats

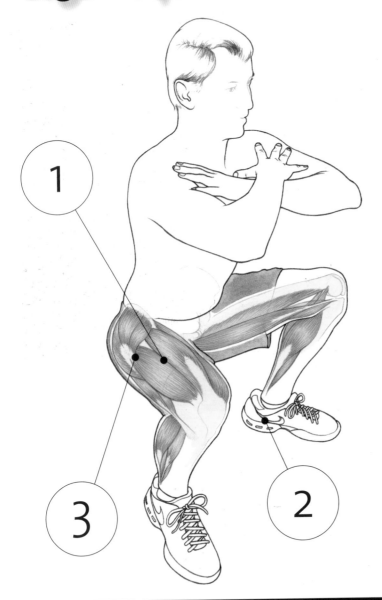

1 Keep knees soft and gently squeeze abs and bum. Tip your hips back as if you are sitting down in a chair, then go down until your upper leg is parallel with the floor. Push back up to the start position.

2 Keep all the weight driving through your heels, as this will maximize the workload in the glutes and hamstrings. Make sure your back stays long and keep knees over your middle toes.

3 As you start to fatigue, focus on keeping your abs and bum muscles engaged as this will protect the lower back. Use your breath to help, releasing breath as you press up.

Muscles Used	How will it improve my cycling?
Primary: quads, glutes, hamstrings, lower back (erector spinae). Secondary: calves.	Muscle strength in your quads and calves can mean the difference between creeping and flitting up a short, steep hill.

Legs – lunges

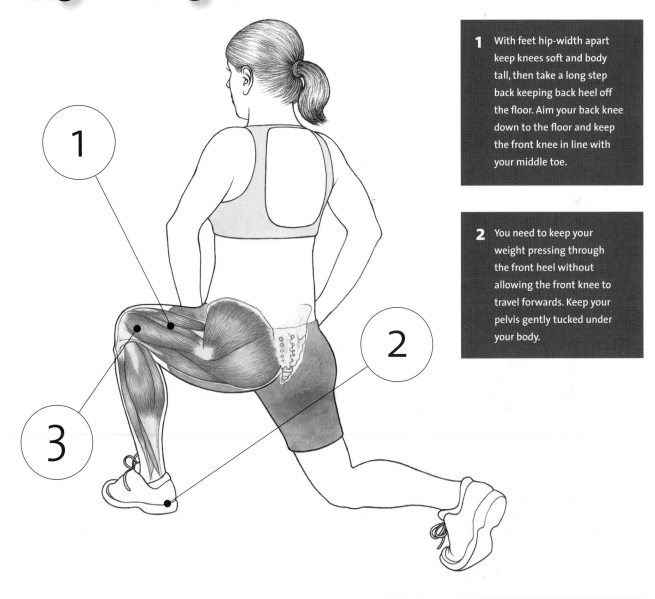

1 With feet hip-width apart keep knees soft and body tall, then take a long step back keeping back heel off the floor. Aim your back knee down to the floor and keep the front knee in line with your middle toe.

2 You need to keep your weight pressing through the front heel without allowing the front knee to travel forwards. Keep your pelvis gently tucked under your body.

3 The feel of the lunge movement is straight down and up. There should be no forward movement. This will keep the pressure on the front knee.

Muscles Used	How will it improve my cycling?
Primary: quads, glutes, hamstrings, calves.	Increased leg strength increases aerobic capacity and time-to-exhaustion. Ride faster with more power and less fatigue.

Legs – hamstring curls

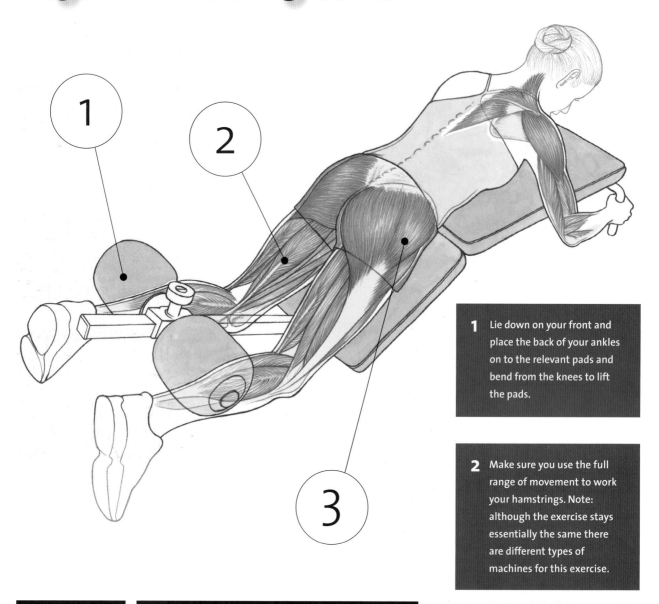

1 Lie down on your front and place the back of your ankles on to the relevant pads and bend from the knees to lift the pads.

2 Make sure you use the full range of movement to work your hamstrings. Note: although the exercise stays essentially the same there are different types of machines for this exercise.

3 Avoid allowing your hips to move up and down. Keep your hips still by pulling in your abs. This will help also help to avoid back injuries.

Muscles Used	How will it improve my cycling?
Primary: hamstrings, glutes.	The muscles of your hamstrings work to extend your hip and bend your knee and are especially important to sustain a smooth pedal stroke.

Legs – bench steps

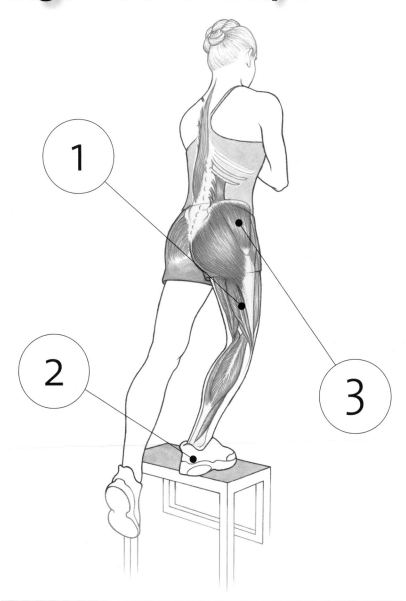

1 Stand about 30cm (about 12 inches) away from a step or bench. Step one foot up before bringing the other leg up, always keeping the foot and knee at a right angle.

2 When stepping onto the bench with your first leg, carefully put the heel down first. This will keep your body secure on the bench and activate the correct muscles.

3 Always keep the body straight and tall. The temptation is to lean forward from the hips. To increase the intensity you can hold weights in each hand.

Muscles Used	How will it improve my cycling?
Primary: Quads, glutes. Secondary: hamstrings, calves.	Strong leg muscles and muscular endurance help prevent fatigue and this freshness will help you to maintain sharp reflexes and your technique.

Legs – calf raises

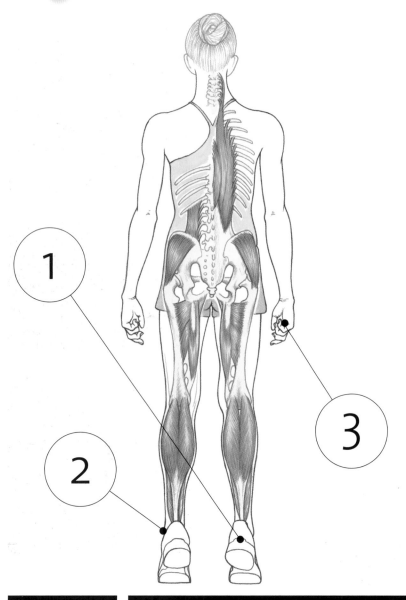

1 Keep feet hip-width apart and your body tall, then rise up high onto the balls of the feet, and lower back to starting position.

2 Keep your ankles in neutral alignment. The temptation is to let your heels fall out to the side. Always keep the whole body lifted and straight.

3 To increase the intensity you can hold a weight in each hand. If no equipment is available simply use cans of food or something heavy and easy to hold.

Muscles Used	How will it improve my cycling?
Primary: calves.	Calf muscles are important because they transmit force from your glutes and quads to your feet and provide power in the lower half of your pedal stroke.

Legs – jump squats

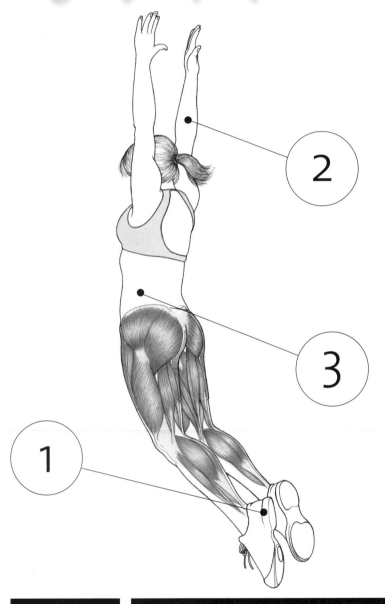

1 This is advanced dynamic work. Take a shallow squat then jump forward pushing equally off both feet to jump as far as you can. Land through a heel-to-toe action and bend the knees on impact to cushion the landing.

2 Take a pause between each rep to steady the body so you are in a strong starting position. You can use your arms to gain momentum, using a natural swing.

3 As with all dynamic work there is a high risk of injury if the exercise is not performed correctly, so as you get tired make sure your abs are gently squeezed in and landings are soft. If you can't maintain this then it's time to stop.

Muscles Used	How will it improve my cycling?
Primary: quads, glutes, hamstrings, lower back. Secondary: calves.	This is a good all-round exercise because it develops your quads, hamstrings, glutes and calves, all of which are important for power on the road.

Shoulders – shoulder press

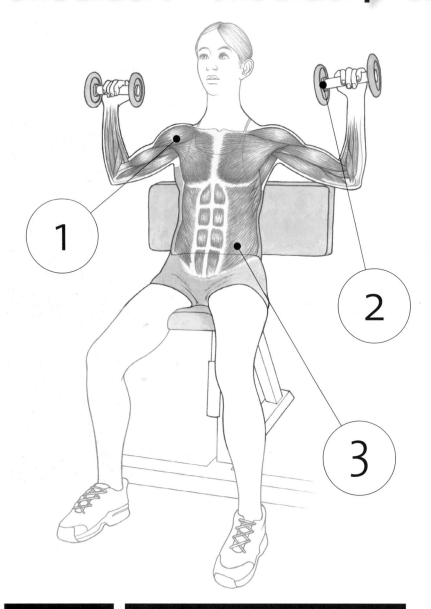

1 Sitting down, ensure elbows are at shoulder height with arms at a right angle and the hands and weight heading up. Push the weights up to the ceiling, and gently bring them together at the top.

2 The weights will move in a slight arc, but keep control and don't allow them to bang into each other at the top.

3 Be very aware of the lower back in this exercise. Do not allow the back to arch. You can combat this by squeezing your abs and gently tucking the pelvis under.

Muscles Used

Primary: shoulders (deltoids).
Secondary: triceps.

How will it improve my cycling?

Shoulders are highly vulnerable to injury because when you fall off your bicycle you naturally follow your instinct by sticking out your arms to protect yourself so develop overall shoulder strength.

* To do this exercise without weights, start in the same position but put both feet on a resistance band and pull round in an arc from your shoulders in the same path to the top as with weights.

Shoulders – rotator cuff

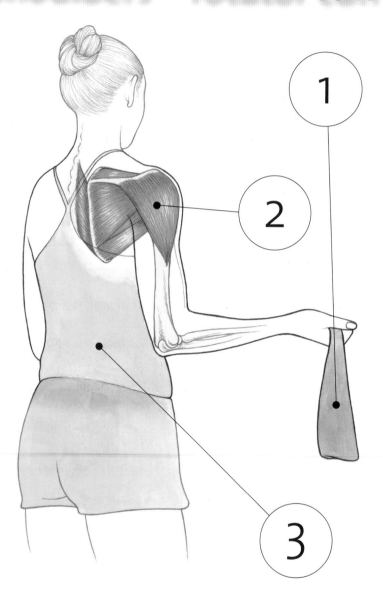

1 Using a resistance band, start with one end of the band tied to a pole and hold the other end in one hand. Ensuring you keep your working elbow close to your body pull your hand across the body at a right angle.

2 While keeping your elbow at a right angle, open your arm outwards from your body so you are squeezing the back of your shoulder.

3 This is a great exercise for keeping the shoulder alignment open. Make sure your posture stays true so you don't allow any movement around your back.

Muscles Used	How will it improve my cycling?
Primary: back of shoulder (rotator cuff).	Extensive riding can leave your shoulders rounded. Without compensating strength exercises like this, such deconditioning can create poor posture and backaches on the bicycle.

Shoulders – bent-over rowing

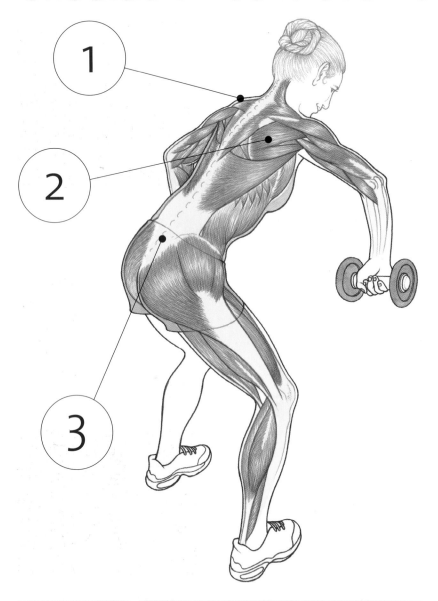

1 Start with the weights down by your knees. Stay in this bent over position and squeeze the weights in towards the belly button in a rowing movement, before straightening your arms to the starting position again.

2 When lifting the weights feel your shoulder blades squeezing together. This will concentrate the workload in the centre of your back.

3 Staying in this position can be tough on your lower back and there is a temptation to curve your lower spine outwards. Avoid this by keeping your pelvis in the correct alignment and squeezing your abs.

Muscles Used	How will it improve my cycling?
Primary: neck, shoulder and back (trapezius). Secondary: biceps.	Strong shoulder muscles help you to stabilize the handlebars when pedalling hard, especially while sprinting and climbing steep hills.

* To do this exercise without weights, start in the same position but put both feet on a resistance band and pull round in an arc from your shoulders in the same path to the top as with weights.

Chest – press-ups

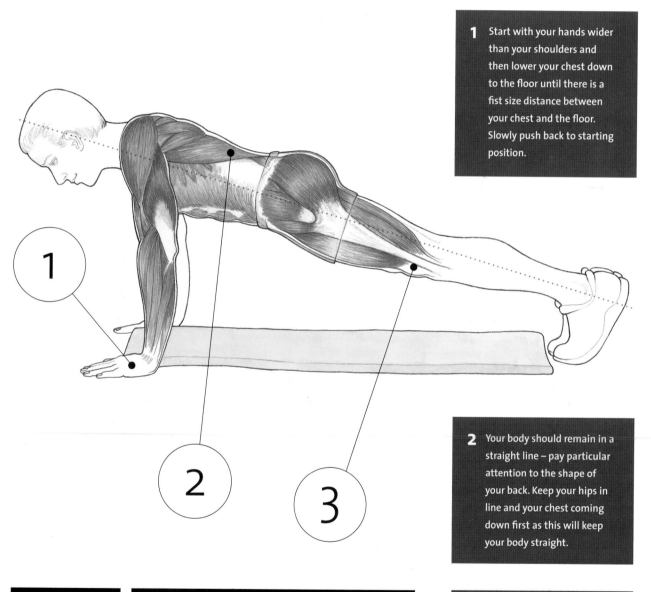

1 Start with your hands wider than your shoulders and then lower your chest down to the floor until there is a fist size distance between your chest and the floor. Slowly push back to starting position.

2 Your body should remain in a straight line – pay particular attention to the shape of your back. Keep your hips in line and your chest coming down first as this will keep your body straight.

3 You can lower your knees down to lower the intensity of the press-up. You should also do this if you feel you are losing your body alignment.

Muscles Used

Primary: pecs.
Secondary: triceps.

How will it improve my cycling?

This exercise imitates the push on the handlebars that is used during technical rides through dips and on uneven terrain like cobblestones.

Arms – bicep curls

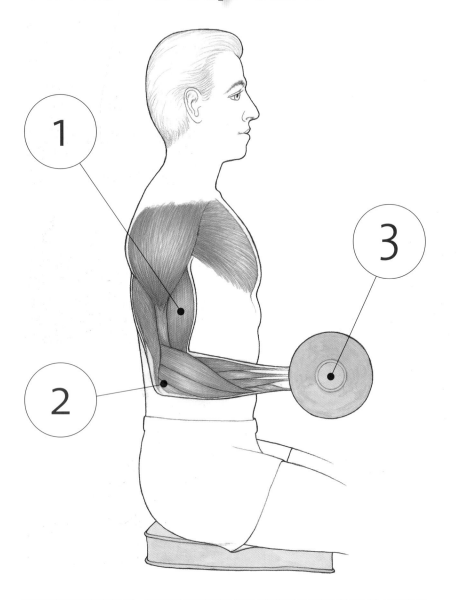

1 Hold the weights with your palms facing forwards while keeping your hands at a natural carrying grip. Bend at the elbow and curl the weights to your chest. Pause briefly then curl back to the horizontal starting position.

2 Keep your elbows close to your body and do not allow them to pull back behind the body alignment.

3 Your hands need to remain strong but soft. If you grip too hard you will feel your forearms work more as opposed to your biceps.

Muscles Used	How will it improve my cycling?
Primary: biceps.	Strong biceps are important for maintaining your core balance on the bicycle. Strong arms help to avoid unnecessary loss of energy.

* To do this exercise without weights, start in the same position but put both feet on a resistance band and pull round in an arc from your shoulders in the same path to the top as with weights.

Arms – tricep dips

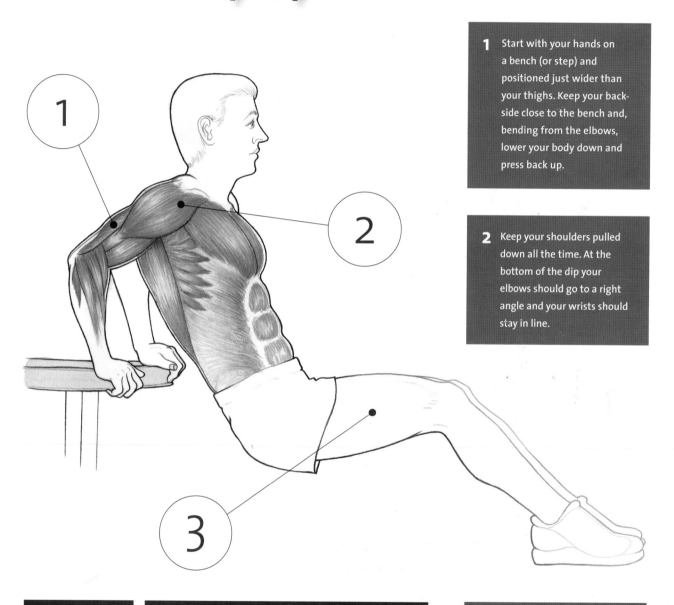

1 Start with your hands on a bench (or step) and positioned just wider than your thighs. Keep your backside close to the bench and, bending from the elbows, lower your body down and press back up.

2 Keep your shoulders pulled down all the time. At the bottom of the dip your elbows should go to a right angle and your wrists should stay in line.

Muscles Used	How will it improve my cycling?
Primary: triceps.	Strong triceps give your body overall strength balance and help with improve your bicycle-handling capabilities.

3 You can make this exercise more intense by straightening your legs and flexing your feet. When doing this keep your backside close to your body.

Core – front plank

1 To get into position place your forearms flat on the floor with your elbows just behind your shoulder alignment. There should be a flat line between the crown of your head, hips and heels. Hold the position for 30 seconds or more.

2 Back alignment is crucial in this exercise. You must maintain the natural curve of your spine by keeping your pelvis centred. Pushing your weight back into your heels can really lengthen your spine.

3 If you cannot maintain the correct alignment, gently lower your knees to the floor. You should do this for a lower intensity option.

Muscles Used

Primary: deep and superficial abs and lower back.

How will it improve my cycling?

Your torso is an integral part of the pedal stroke. A strong torso provides the rigidity to deliver maximum power from your quads to the pedals.

Core – side plank

1 To get into position place one hand on the floor with your elbow in a direct line under your shoulder. Your hips should be stacked one on top of the other. Then lift up as if you a drawing away from a flame until your body is in position as per the illustration. Hold for 30 seconds or more.

2 As with the front plank the key is body alignment. Your back must maintain its natural curve – lengthen your legs as the will help to keep your back long.

3 A lower intensity alternative of this exercise is to bend your knees at a right angle so your feet are behind and lift up on your arm while balancing on your knees. This can be used if your shoulders are weak.

Muscles Used

Primary: side abs, deep and superficial abs and lower back.

How will it improve my cycling?

Your body's core, which includes the back and abdominal muscles, can be a weak link, especially if you specialize in time trialling. Many riders lose significant pedal power because of a weak lower back and abdominal muscles.

Core – sit-ups

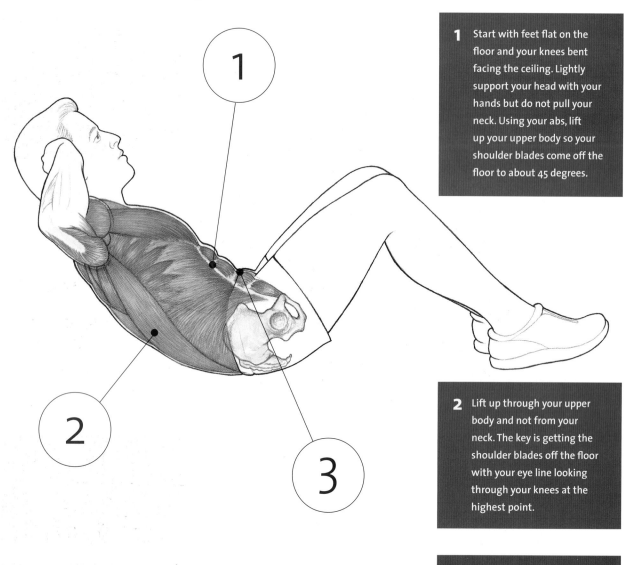

1 Start with feet flat on the floor and your knees bent facing the ceiling. Lightly support your head with your hands but do not pull your neck. Using your abs, lift up your upper body so your shoulder blades come off the floor to about 45 degrees.

2 Lift up through your upper body and not from your neck. The key is getting the shoulder blades off the floor with your eye line looking through your knees at the highest point.

3 To get the best results keep pulling your belly button gently back towards the spine. For increased intensity and to improve balance, this exercise can be done with the base of your back balanced on an exercise ball.

Muscles Used	How will it improve my cycling?
Primary: superficial abs.	The trunk, which includes the abdominal muscles, is a weak link for most cyclists. You need substantial torso support to resist the enormous forces that your leg muscles generate.

Core – shoulder bridge

1 Lie flat on your back with the soles of your feet on the floor and knees bent up to the ceiling. Slowly roll up through your pelvis then ease back to the starting position.

2 To increase the intensity you can hold the movement at the top then extend one leg up to the ceiling. Alternate legs.

3 At the top of the movement your shoulders, hips and knees should all be in a line. When rolling up and down, imagine your spine as a bicycle chain and roll through each link one at a time.

Muscles Used

Primary: glutes, hamstrings, lower back, abs.

How will it improve my cycling?

Because of the bent-over position on a bicycle, your back muscles are continuously under pressure. This stress can cause a lot of trouble if it isn't conditioned and trained to withstand the ongoing effort.

Core – leg raises

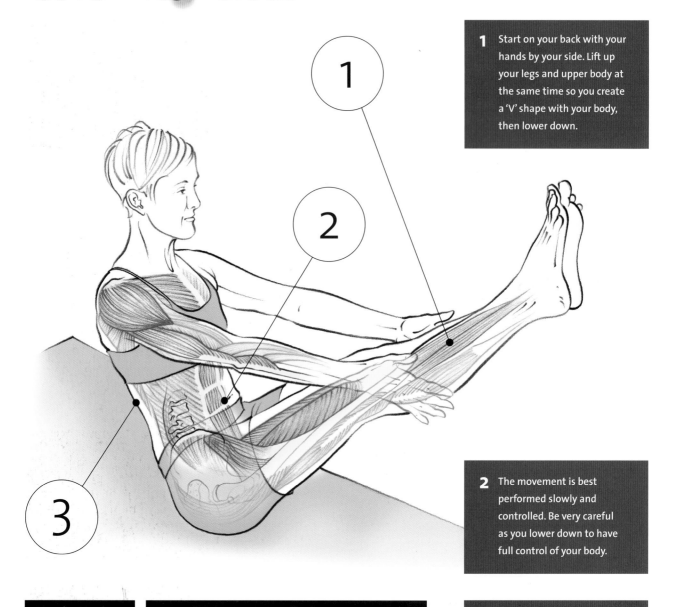

1 Start on your back with your hands by your side. Lift up your legs and upper body at the same time so you create a 'V' shape with your body, then lower down.

2 The movement is best performed slowly and controlled. Be very careful as you lower down to have full control of your body.

3 This is a tough exercise and performed incorrectly can cause injury to the back. A good option to start with is to keep the knees bent as you come up.

Muscles Used	How will it improve my cycling?
Primary: top of leg and abs, hip flexors.	The constant effect of the power of your legs causes to overwork your lower back muscles which results in the so-called 'S' curve in the back. This exercise will help to correct it.

Core – back raises

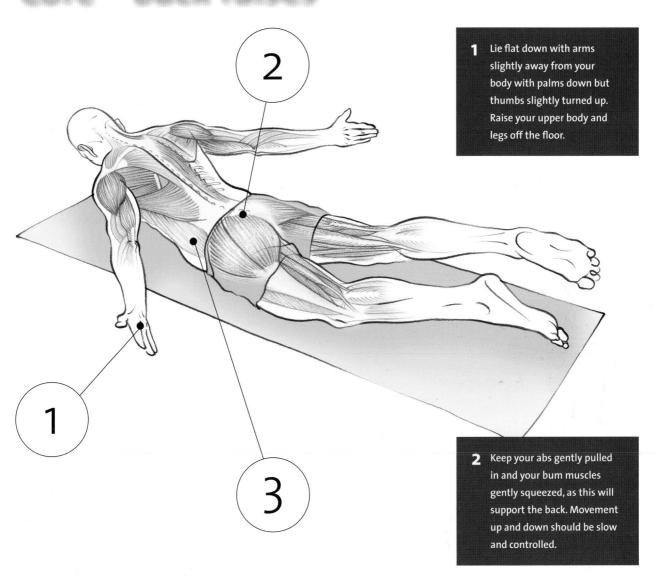

1 Lie flat down with arms slightly away from your body with palms down but thumbs slightly turned up. Raise your upper body and legs off the floor.

2 Keep your abs gently pulled in and your bum muscles gently squeezed, as this will support the back. Movement up and down should be slow and controlled.

3 If you want more support for your back place your hands under your shoulders for support and push up from the floor. Use as much or as little pressure on the hands as you need.

Muscles Used	How will it improve my cycling?
Primary: lower back.	This exercise is great for cyclists because it helps to strengthen your lower back muscles and hamstrings, which are especially important during time trialling and climbing.

Back – prone back extension

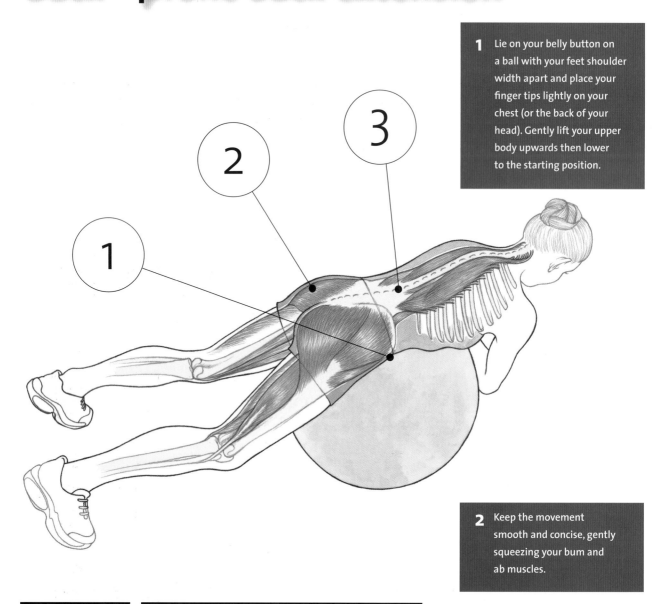

1 Lie on your belly button on a ball with your feet shoulder width apart and place your finger tips lightly on your chest (or the back of your head). Gently lift your upper body upwards then lower to the starting position.

2 Keep the movement smooth and concise, gently squeezing your bum and ab muscles.

3 Rolling further forward on the ball can make the exercise more intense but be careful as this can put more pressure on the lower back.

Muscles Used

Primary: lower back.

How will it improve my cycling?

You should avoid having tight hip muscles and weak back muscles because this could easily lead to knee pain. This exercise will help you to strengthen your back muscles.

Workout programme – beginners

Sets x2, reps x8-12 (sit-ups, core raises, back raises x15 reps), 1 min recovery between exercises.
Planks: aim for 30 second holds (reduce if losing technique).

To find your ideal weight for each exercise you should be able to complete the reps but just about hit failure on the final rep. As a guide, the heaviest weight you would use would be for your larger muscle groups (eg glutes and quads used in squats) and the lightest weight you would use would be for your smaller muscle groups (eg biceps in bicep curls).

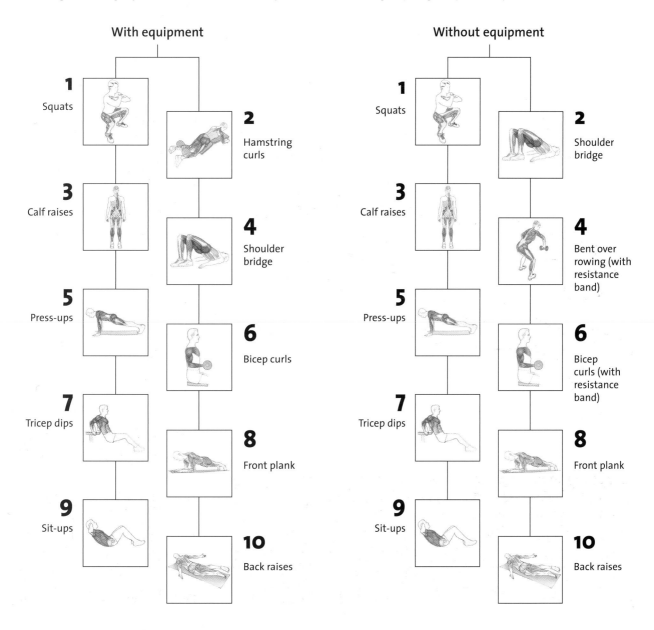

With equipment

1 Squats
2 Hamstring curls
3 Calf raises
4 Shoulder bridge
5 Press-ups
6 Bicep curls
7 Tricep dips
8 Front plank
9 Sit-ups
10 Back raises

Without equipment

1 Squats
2 Shoulder bridge
3 Calf raises
4 Bent over rowing (with resistance band)
5 Press-ups
6 Bicep curls (with resistance band)
7 Tricep dips
8 Front plank
9 Sit-ups
10 Back raises

Workout programme – intermediate

Sets x2, reps x10-15 (core raises x20 reps).
Planks: aim for 45 second holds (reduce if losing technique).

To find your ideal weight for each exercise you should be able to complete the reps but just about hit failure on the final rep. As a guide the heaviest weight you would use would be for your larger muscle groups (eg glutes and quads used in squats) and the lightest weight you would use would be for your smaller muscle groups (eg shoulders in bent-over rowing).

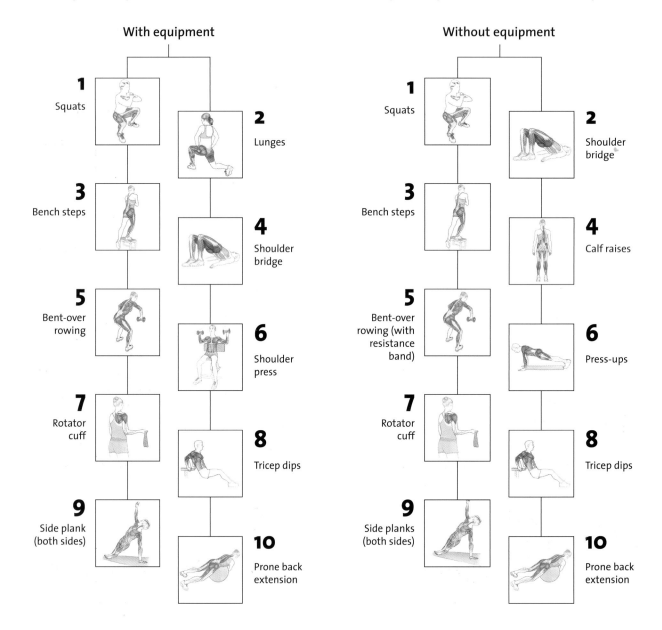

With equipment

1 Squats
2 Lunges
3 Bench steps
4 Shoulder bridge
5 Bent-over rowing
6 Shoulder press
7 Rotator cuff
8 Tricep dips
9 Side plank (both sides)
10 Prone back extension

Without equipment

1 Squats
2 Shoulder bridge
3 Bench steps
4 Calf raises
5 Bent-over rowing (with resistance band)
6 Press-ups
7 Rotator cuff
8 Tricep dips
9 Side planks (both sides)
10 Prone back extension

Workout programme – advanced

Sets x3, reps x12-15 (core raises x30 reps).

Planks: aim for 1 min to 1 min and 30 seconds holds (reduce if losing technique).

To find your ideal weight for each exercise you should be able to complete the reps but just about hit failure on the final rep. As a guide, the heaviest weight you would use would be for your larger muscle groups (eg glutes and quads used in squats) and the lightest weight you would use would be for your smaller muscle groups (eg shoulders in bent-over rowing).

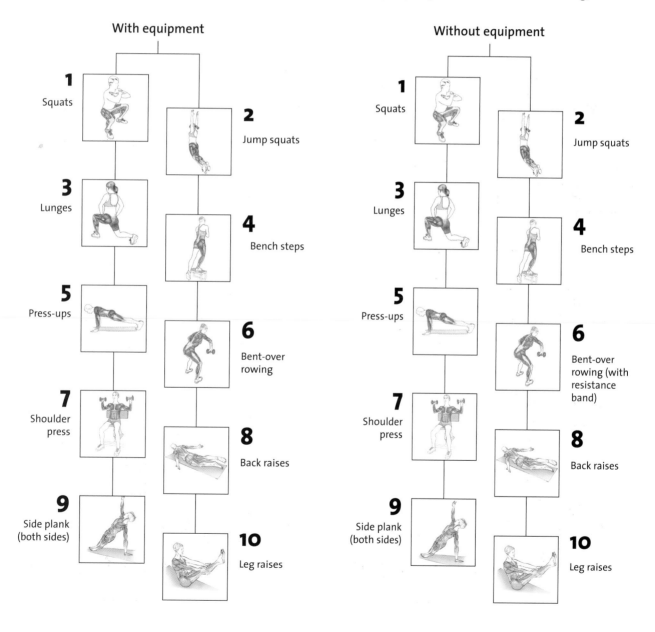

With equipment

1 Squats
2 Jump squats
3 Lunges
4 Bench steps
5 Press-ups
6 Bent-over rowing
7 Shoulder press
8 Back raises
9 Side plank (both sides)
10 Leg raises

Without equipment

1 Squats
2 Jump squats
3 Lunges
4 Bench steps
5 Press-ups
6 Bent-over rowing (with resistance band)
7 Shoulder press
8 Back raises
9 Side plank (both sides)
10 Leg raises

nutrition

// HEALTHIER // LIVELIER
// MORE ENERGETIC

The basics

Food and nutrition are the basic elements for a correct training regime in any sport. Think of your body as if it were a car – it could have the most powerful engine, the most aerodynamic shape or the best design but it would never run without its fuel. Food is the natural fuel for your body.

Food can be divided into four basic groups: **carbohydrates, proteins, fats** and **liquids** and each one of them is equally important in running our body, giving it energy, stamina, resistance and self-recovery. Each one of these elements is essential to our nutrition and is absolutely harmless to our health and body if taken in the right amounts, balanced in combination with all the others.

Carbohydrates are the fuel for your muscles. They provide the energy for your muscles to work.

Proteins build and repair muscles whenever they have been stressed during exercise.

Fats are energy stores for your body and help the correct functioning of the cells and maintain your body's temperature.

Liquids maintain the right body fluid concentration and expel toxins.

A correct combination of each one of the above-mentioned elements, adjusted depending on the sport and your body's response, will provide you with the correct nutrition needed, both for training and competition.

A basic diet for an athlete or an active person (someone who trains three times a week for more that 60 minutes per training session) should amount to a daily intake of 3,000–4,500 calories per day, according to the sport and the amount of training. This might seem a lot more than what you heard in your sports club or while chatting when jogging but remember that this diet is not planned in order to make you lose weight but to give you an under-standing of what your body needs to perform at its best while under the athletic stress.

If you eat the right foods at the right time, plan your weekly diet with the same care you use to plan your training, weight will never be a problem and you will understand how a correct diet (as a plan to correctly feed your body, instead of a rush into weight loss) will drastically improve your life as well as your athletic performance

Nutrition in sports is as important as the exercise. Again, your body,

as a car, needs the right fuel to perform at its best.

There are four key steps you need to understand before planning your diet:

1. Do not get too hungry as it will make you take the wrong dietary choices and swallow whatever you can find. Have at least five meals a day, calibrating the amounts at each meal.
2. Eat at least three different kinds of foods at each meal as mono-eating will make your body incapable of digesting correctly what you don't usually eat. Choosing different kinds of vegetables, fish and meat, will provide your body with different vitamins and minerals.
3. Always balance the food elements at each meal. Every meal should be based on carbohydrates combined with proteins and fats (amounts change from person to person; but a good starting base is a balance of 50 per cent carbo-hydrates, 30 per cent proteins and 20 per cent fats).
4. Try to choose foods in their natural state. A banana is better than an energy bar and an orange is better than orange juice for instance.

Assess your diet

People tend to be obsessed by their body shape. It is a normal feeling given the kind of images the media world sends us every day. When you assess your ideal diet, try to forget about your shape and think realistically for a moment about what goals you want to achieve athletically. By doing so you will be more focused on understanding, planning and applying the correct diet to everyday life.

First question: do you have breakfast?

Eat breakfast every morning. If you train early in the morning try to wake up half-an-hour before you normally would just to make sure you eat a good amount of food for breakfast. If waking up earlier is going to be impossible, try to eat more carbohydrates the night before, and top up the next morning with some snack. It's very important for you to eat something one hour before training, as it will guarantee the sugars flow in your blood, while the muscles will use the energy stored during the night.

Avoid hyper-protein breakfasts. Remember that every meal should be based around carbohydrates. A little sample of ideal food for breakfast would be:

- Porridge with cottage cheese or ricotta cheese and some nuts.
- A cup of milk or yoghurt over a bowl of cereals with a banana and some raisins. Remember that all-bran cereals tend to be stressful for the bowels, which is inappropriate for training and competition. Also avoid sugar-coated cereals.
- A sandwich made with two slices of whole-grain bread and 60 grams of smoked salmon (you could add a some light cream cheese) and an orange or a glass of orange juice.
- Muesli with yoghurt and one piece of fruit.

If you feel the need for a boost of caffeine, feel free to drink it, as it would not interfere with your training (although it gives stomach acidity to some people). No person is the same, which means it's up to you to find your right intake by calibrating and testing day after day to find the right proportions and taste to suit you.

Second question: do you snack after training?

Remember that eating and drinking after training is the only way you can start to refuel your empty muscles. You can choose what kind of snack you should have, depending on the amount of energy spent and the length of the interval before your next training session. This is the moment where you really train your muscles to intake and store more and more glycogen.

You have two options: either you go for a low or a high GI snack. GI is the acronym for Glycemic Index which is a measure of the effects of carbohydrates on sugar levels. Carbohydrates can be released into the blood slowly (in that case they have a low GI) or quickly (high GI). Although important for the control of illnesses like diabetes, the control of the GI is something that most athletes don't really worry about. What you must decide is the kind of recovery you want from your diet.

If you have two training sessions in one day, or another training session the morning after, then you might want to consider a high GI recovery, choosing food like corn flakes, white bread, watermelon or baked potatoes. On the other hand, it's been shown that a low or medium GI recovery, because of its slower release of sugars, will be more effective in the long run, using food like fruits, vegetables, whole-grain breads, pasta, milk and yoghurt.

Remember that gulping down gallons of protein shakes after training will be almost useless.

You need mainly carbohydrates to refuel your muscles and only some proteins to recover the stressed muscles and help new ones to grow.

Third question: do you ever go hungry during the day?
If you do sometimes go hungry in the day you need adjust your plans to make sure this doesn't happen. Make sure you plan your meals and snacks beforehand by experimenting with your meals for a few days and organize your day around the food you know you will need.

Ideally you should have one substantial breakfast before leaving your house, one snack no longer than four hours after breakfast (between 10.00 and 11.00 for most people), one lunch (if you think it would be better then prepare it the night before, in order to avoid rushing into eating any food you find in the shops when hungry). The have another snack three to four hours later, a good dinner (try to avoid pasta, rice and bread for dinner, unless preparing for a competition or the night before the competition itself) and one last evening snack.

Fourth question: do you find yourself fatigued during training?
There could be different reasons for being fatigued during training.

- A low glycogen storage. The glycogen has been burned and you are now using your proteins and fats as fuel, provoking your blood to carry ketones to your brain. In this case you should eat more carbohydrates before training and more carbohydrates after training, in order to teach your muscles to store as much glycogen as possible.
- Dehydration. A lack of liquids means your body can't cool down properly, endangering the health of you cells and making the expulsion of carbon dioxide and lactic acid more difficult.

Carbohydrates

One of the many myths you may have read is that carbohydrates are fattening. This is untrue. Fats are fattening, carbohydrates are the basic fuel you need to eat in order to have enough energy in your muscles. In a sports diet carbohydrates are an absolute must of your nutrition requirements.

Carbohydrates can be divided into two groups: simple and complex. Simple carbohydrates are monosaccharides (single-sugar molecules: fructose, glucose and galactose) and disaccharides (double-sugar molecules: table sugar, milk sugar, honey and refined syrups). Fruits and vegetables contain many different kinds of carbohydrates, which is one of the reasons why your diet should include a good variety of vegetables and fruits.

During digestion your stomach turns the sugars and carbohydrates into glucose, before the latter is then turned into a polymer (a chain of five or more sugar molecules) called glycogen. Glycogen is the key to your energy levels. Glycogen gets stored in your muscles and your liver, supplying your body with the right amount of energy for your training or your competition.

While the glycogen stored in your muscles will function as an energy reserve to move your body and train your muscles, the one stored in your liver will provide a slow-release of sugars into your bloodstream, guaranteeing a constant amount of sugars to your brain. This is important, because the sugars in your brain will influence your performance drastically.

Did you ever hear about, or ever hit the infamous 'wall'? The wall is something many professional athletes have hit during their career. It's a moment during which you become sure you are not going to make it to the finish. The wall is not a metaphysical concept, it is simply the moment when you have no more sugars flowing to your brain. Having the right amount of glycogen stored in both your muscles and your liver will help you avoid the wall.

What is the main difference between the different sugars, then? While refined sugars, soft drinks and energy drinks will only provide an energy supply, vegetables and fruits will supply, along with different amounts of glucose, also vitamins and minerals which will help spark and run your body engine in the correct way.

Always try to eat foods in their natural state. Whole-wheat breads, brown rice, brown pasta, as all the nutritional elements you will find in unrefined products, are more valuable than the ones you will find in refined ones. The same concept can be applied to cooked carbohydrates – it is preferable to undercook vegetables, in order for them to retain the vitamins and minerals contained in them along with the sugars and starches. This leads to a very important point you should be aware of. Your muscles need to be trained not only through exercise, but also by making them capable of storing the biggest amount of glycogen possible. How do you do that? By eating the right carbohydrates in the right amount.

During training you put your muscles under stress in order to grow them and make them stronger. At the same time, by supplying them with the right amount of carbohydrates, you will teach them to store more glycogen.

In 100 grams of untrained muscle you can store only 13 grams of glycogen but the same amount of trained muscle will store about 32 grams, while a muscle trained to be loaded with carbohydrates will be able to store between 35 and 40 grams. Needless to say, the latter is the muscle that will perform better and for longer.

Carbohydrates

1 Unrefined food will have a better nutritional value than the refined ones. Wild rice, whole-wheat breads, brown pasta, popcorn (unbuttered), oats and porridge, raw fruits and vegetables, etc.

2 Always make sure that any meal you take during the day is based around carbohydrates. Try to think in terms of the proportions stated above (50-30-20).

3 Vary your food as much as possible. A good way is to plan your meals by colour (green leaves or broccoli, tomatoes, peppers, carrots, oranges, apples, blueberries, etc).

4 Always make sure that before and after training you have the right amount of carbohydrates to restore your energy levels and sugars in your bloodstream. Once the glycogen is used up your body will start burning your fat as an energy supplement. Although this is the basic concept of how to trim down your stomach, bear in mind that such a process is detrimental to your performance, as your bloodstream will carry ketons to your brain instead of sugars, amplifying your tiredness and affecting your mood.

Proteins

Let's start by refuting another myth: proteins do not make you stronger, exercise does. There is always a magic aura around words such as proteins and amino acids, believed to be the mysterious ingredients to a muscular body. Don't worry, it's not so mysterious.

Proteins have many different roles in your body. They help build new muscles, repair those stressed by exercise, are the reason your hair and nails grow, energize your immune system and, above all, help replace red blood cells. A protein-based diet is useless. Drinking protein shakes, eating too many egg whites, or stuffing yourself with chicken breast will lead to poor results. An over-intake of proteins can be useless, even counterproductive. Your body can store only a certain amount of protein or amino acids and if you exceed this they will be either burned for energy (a scarce amount if compared to carbohydrates) when the body runs out, or stored as glycogen or fat. There are two main problems you can face if following a diet with too much protein.

1. It will prevent you from eating the right amount of carbohydrates, lowering the amount of energy stored in your muscles.
2. It will break down into urea,

an organic compound your body eliminates through urine. People who eat too many proteins will need to increase their fluid intake to eliminate as much urea as possible, leading to frequent visits to the toilet.

By eating too many proteins you also increase the chance of eating excessive fats (through meats, and condiments) that your body will store. The correct amount of protein an athlete can digest varies but as a rule of thumb, is calculated to be between 1.2 and 1.6 grams per body weight kilogram per day. That is usually less than your daily intake by only eating meat, fish, dairy products or legumes. The ideal intake would be a daily total of about 150g to 200g, adding the proteins you should get from two servings of low-fat dairy products (milk, yoghurt and cheese) per day.

Meats can be divided in three kinds: white meats, red meats and fish. An ideal sports diet should include all kinds of meats in your weekly plan.

- Fish is the best option as the fats it contains are unsaturated (including the famous Omega-3), so is a better choice than the saturated fats commonly found in meats and dairy products.
- White meat is preferable to red meat as it usually contains less fat

(if it is either breast or properly skinned thigh and drumsticks).
- Lean red meat, although not the healthiest option, should be eaten between three and four times per week. Red meat contains iron and zinc and iron is an essential part of haemoglobin, a protein that transports oxygen to your muscles and brain. If you are missing the right amount of iron you could suffer fatigue and exhaustion. Zinc is a mineral that plays a big role in removing carbon dioxide from your muscles when you are exercising. A good red meat is venison as it contains a lower quantity of saturated fat.

With dairy products you should eat low-fat. Semi-skimmed milk and yoghurt are close to the ideal intake percentage (they contain a percentage of 40 per cent carbohydrates, 35 per cent proteins, 25 per cent fats), so are a perfect snack. It's an easy way to eat proteins and also supply vitamin D and calcium and the right amount of potassium, phosphorus and riboflavin. Potassium and phosphorus help your body in metabolizing the calcium to strengthen your bones, while riboflavin is a vitamin that helps your body to transform the food into energy.

Proteins

1 Choose fish before white meat or red meat, but make sure you eat all three kinds during the week.

2 Include proteins in every meal.

3 You can find all the proteins you need in the food you eat – you don't need to use shakes, bars or pills.

4 Try to eat low-fat dairy products at least once, preferably twice a day.

5 Do not overfeed yourself with proteins, as it is useless.

Fats

Fat is as important in your diet as any other food element. Fat helps provide the temperature regulation of your body, helps the health of skin and hair and provides a safety coating for your internal organs.

The most important thing is to know what kinds of fat you should eat and in what quantities. Fats can be divided into hard fats and soft fats. Hard fats are the fats that come in the form of meat lard, chicken skin or butter, while soft fats, the ones you should favour in your diet, are in the form of olive oil and canola oil.

As mentioned earlier, calories from fat should correspond to about 20 per cent of your diet. The most important thing to remember is to stay away from Hydrogenated Trans

Fats, which are a very unhealthy result of a chemical process that adds hydrogen to both mono and polyunsaturated fats.

Don't be afraid of eating fats during your resting periods. Many people think if you don't exercise your muscles will turn into fat and you will gain weight. That is untrue. Muscles and fat are two distinct components of your body and you will only gain weight by taking more calories from fat than the ones you are burning, which, in the doses that have been mentioned before, is very unlikely.

You might have seen people in the gym torturing their abs, hoping to lose their belly by over-exercising the part closest to it. What you need to understand is that you lose

your excessive fat by exercising the whole body and consuming the calories that you have taken. Let's put it this way: if you want to lose fat, you need to grow your muscles (in the whole body), as bigger muscles consume more calories. Don't try to over-stress specific areas of your body, as this is useless.

Remember that fats are what gives taste to your food, helping to make it more favourable to your palate. As you are making an effort to stick to a dietary plan for your athletic training, try to enjoy it as much as possible, adding the right amount of healthy fats to your meals.

Fats

1   Olive oil is a monounsaturated fat and is the best choice. Always try to buy extra-virgin olive oil and use it to cook and dress any food you want. The ideal amount should be around two teaspoons for each meal.

2   Nuts – like walnuts, almonds, pistachios, macadamia, Brazilian nuts, pine kernels, olives – are also a good choice for fat intake. Each one of them is a different size and contains a different amount of fat, so it's important to weigh them so you know approximately how many you need. For example: cashew nuts, peanuts, almonds, pine kernels, require a dose of nine grams per meal while walnuts, macadamias, hazelnuts, pecans and pistachios are about seven to eight grams per meal. For avocado and green olives allow a bit more (about 18 grams for the avocado and 30 grams for the olives).

3   Fish oil is another good choice, as it is rich in healthy fats. However, not many people like the taste and it would be a pity to waste a whole meal because of it.

Liquids

Water is the base of life. Your body is made in the most part by liquids and any loss of liquids has to be quickly restored.

Water does the following.

- It keeps your blood liquid, helping the correct transportation of oxygen, glucose and fat, while taking away carbon dioxide and lactic acid.
- It helps keep your body cool by absorbing heat from your muscles, sweating the heat out, cooling the skin through evaporating sweat and allowing the cooled down epidermis to cool the blood that cools down the organs. It's a positive vicious cycle.

Thirst is the most common sensation our body delivers to make us aware that we need to restore our balance. This sensation becomes more complicated when we deal with sports however.

There are many variables to be taken into consideration when you are exercising. There is the level of preparation, the weather, the fact your mind is focused on a goal, your body is too well trained or, because of the water on your body, you don't feel the heat. Bear in mind that, while exercising, your brain will communicate 'thirst' to you when you have already lost about one per cent of liquids and then it might be too late to rehydrate yourself. At that point your heart is beating more than needed, burning more glycogen than it should. At a two per cent loss you are officially dehydrated and at three per cent your body could be impaired in continuing the task.

The secret is to plan your drinking as well as your eating. Evaluate the amount of liquids you lose during a training session. To do so, weigh yourself naked before the training and right after, before drinking. The difference in weight will tell you the amount of liquids you lost. Your urine should always be a pale yellow; if it is dark and dense it means that there are too many metabolic wastes compared to the amount of water.

It takes between eight and 12 hours before your body becomes fully rehydrated so always plan your drinking during both your everyday life and training. By sweating you not only lose liquids but also electrolytes such as magnesium, potassium, sodium and calcium.

Always start you training session fully rehydrated from the session before by drinking between five and eight millilitres per kilo of your body weight. You can add sodium to your drink or chose a sodium enhanced drink, as it might help retain the water in your body.

You can use sodium in food and beverages after you training if you need to rehydrate quickly for a second session (up to 12 hours after the first one). Drinking between 30 per cent and 50 per cent more fluids than the ones you lost during exercise should be enough to re-establish the right concentration of liquids in your body.

Try to stay away from alcohol as much as possible. It causes strong dehydration as it is a potent diuretic and it would make you waste more liquids than you should. Also remember alcohol is a depressant and it suppresses drastically your motor skills along with your mood.

Pre- and post-competition planning

Before the competition

Your pre-competition training should be winding down (tapering) in the few days before the event (see Training programmes page 140). This is because your muscles need time to recover from hard exercise. During this time, while you are reducing your training load you should be re-establishing the glycogen in your muscles, rehydrating yourself and mending the stressed muscles by eating some proteins.

Try to interpret your pre-competition training as a final rehearsal for the real event. Some people think that stuffing themselves with pasta the night before the competition will be enough but things are a bit more complicated than that.

During training you will have taught your muscles to store a good amount of glycogen in order to have a good reserve in every training session. The more you train your muscles with exercise, the more glycogen your muscles will be able to store, if educated to receive it.

From one or two weeks before your competition you should slowly increase the amount of carbohydrates by about 100 grams per day. The day before the competition

itself you should start loading your body with carbohydrates from breakfast time.

Every athlete reacts differently to a competition. Some have no problem having a good dinner the night before – others find it difficult to digest because of the excitement or worry. Therefore, start loading yourself with carbohydrates from breakfast. And, if you feel like eating dinner try to vary the type of carbohydrates as much as you can. Pasta by itself might do the trick, but remember that fruits and vegetables contain slow sugar-releasing carbohydrates and they will help for endurance the day after. Avoid bran flakes or anything that you know could lead to stomach problems.

Cycling is a good sport when compared to many others (such as running for instance), as it is much easier to carry liquids and food, which means you don't have to stop to refill your muscles and re-balance your liquids. When training you should plan ahead and carry what you need in terms of refuelling for that session.

On the morning of the competition, according to the time the event starts, there are few rules you need to follow.

- Make sure you wake up in the morning with the right fluid balance. You can easily determine it by the colour of your urine.

- Start by having a big glass of water and breakfast or, if the competition is too early to have breakfast, make sure you load some more carbohydrates one hour before the event. This will make sure that your liver will produce enough sugar to be delivered to your brain throughout the duration of the competition.

- Drink your water between one to two hours before the race so you can expel it before the race starts.

After the competition

As you will have seen, after the event you need to let your body recover by rebalancing the glycogen and the fluids. Take advantage of the first hour after the event, as it will be the period when you body will assimilate all the nutrients best.

Carbohydrates mixed with a little protein is the best option to have both glycogen delivered to your muscles while reducing the emission of cortisol, the hormone that breaks down your muscles during exercise.

According to whether you will have a short or a long time before the next competition, you will have to find the right way to fully recover your muscles and blood. Swimming often faces you with the problem of back-to-back events and recovering has to be planned carefully.

Different athletes prefer different solutions according to their experience. The main thing is to plan a good nutrition schedule. If you know you will have to face three competitions in 40 hours, you might want to plan your diet starting from the week before, in such way that it will be faster to recover between the events.

If you have two events back to back you want to make sure you will recover immediately after the first one by over-loading yourself with high-GI carbohydrates and liquids that will restore not only the fluids but also the electrolytes (some sport drinks do that). Try to drink as much as possible and judge the level of rehydration from the colour of your urine and comparing your weight before and after the event. If you happen to have more than two competitions in a span of more than two days, keep in mind that low-GI carbohydrates have been proven to be more effective in the long run.

If you have enough time to recover after the event (one week), make sure you rebalance your fluids and have a little snack combining carbo-hydrates and proteins in the usual balance and then take your time, by simply starting the nutritional plan where you left it before the prepa-ration to the competition.

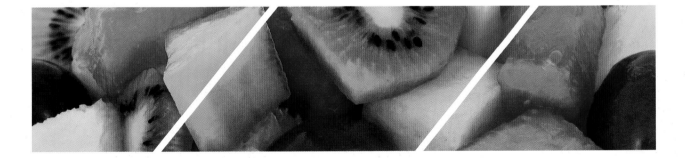

Recipes

OATS, RICOTTA AND PISTACHIOS

Ingredients
- *50 grams rolled oats*
- *140 grams of ricotta cheese*
- *8-10 pistachios, no shells*
- *Pinch of salt or honey*

Preparation Boil the oats in water until reaching your preferred consistency. In a bowl, mix the cooked oats, the ricotta cheese and pistachios. Add either a pinch of salt or half teaspoon of honey, depending on whether you prefer savoury or sweet. This is a perfect balanced snack, which combines proteins, carbohydrates and fat.

COTTAGE CHEESE WITH WARM BLUBERRY AND WALNUTS

Ingredients
- *220 grams of blueberries*
- *1 teaspoon of fructose*
- *70 grams of low-fat cottage cheese*
- *3 walnuts*

Preparation Warm the blueberries in a saucepan over low heat with fructose and a little bit of water and keep stirring gently until the berries are softened. Place the cottage cheese in a bowl and pour the fruits over it. Sprinkle with the crumbled walnuts. Perfect as a snack.

STUFFED SQUID

Ingredients
- *1 big squid (200 grams cleaned – keep the tentacles)*
- *2 teaspoons of chopped parsley and a little chopped garlic*
- *250 grams of grated fresh whole-grain bread or whole-grain breadcrumbs*
- *30 grams of grated Parmesan cheese*
- *1 tablespoon of olive oil*

Preparation Keep the squid body intact. For the filling: chop the tentacles and add them to a bowl along with the parsley, garlic, fresh breadcrumbs and Parmesan. Start pounding the mixture with your hands and add water and oil as needed. Fill the squid with the mix and close it with a toothpick. Put it in the oven for 30 minutes, using any leftover paste to coat the squid. Serve with a side of salad or a piece of fruit cut up.

BUTTER-FREE EGGS FLORENTINE

Ingredients
- *300 grams of spinach*
- *White wine vinegar*
- *35 grams of cottage cheese*
- *2 slices of whole-grain bread, toasted*
- *2 eggs, poached*
- *Salt and pepper to taste*
- *Grated Parmesan cheese or shredded mild Cheddar cheese*

Preparation Boil spinach until lightly soft. Mix a teaspoon of vinegar to the cottage cheese and mix well. Place spinach over the two slices of toasted bread. Arrange cooked, drained eggs over the top of the spinach then pour the cottage cheese over the eggs. Sprinkle with salt, pepper and grated Parmesan cheese.

SPICY OATS WITH GRILLED CHICKEN BREAST (OR VENISON STEAK)

Ingredients
- *3 teaspoons olive oil*
- *1/2 red onion*
- *Pinch of chilli powder, pinch of paprika, 1 bay leaf*
- *1 garlic clove*
- *350 grams of raw oats (in grains)*
- *Grilled chicken breast or 120 gram venison steak*
- *Parsley*

Preparation Mix olive oil and 3 tablespoons of water in a cooking pan. Chop up the onion and cook it in the oily water adding chilli powder, paprika, the bay leaf and garlic until golden. Add oats and let them roast a bit. Then add water and let them cook for 30 minutes. While it's cooking grill the chicken breast or venison steak. Serve with a sprinkle of chopped parsley.

training programmes

// PLANNING // PREPARING // READY TO RACE

The basics

This is a 20-week training programme designed for elite amateur cyclists who are competing at international level. The programme can be used as it is and if you are an athlete at that level it will prepare you for the challenging racing season. You will need to time the start of your programme depending on when the racing season starts in your continent.

This programme follows the principles of periodization by systematically varying the volume, intensity and recovery of the various training phases. If you have been racing for only a few years or want to compete at only the national level, then you reduce the volume by around 30-40 per cent. The same applies to junior cyclists (ages 16-18) who want to race at the highest national and international level. If you have lots of work, college or family commitments and you are just beginning to race or who want to race at the regional level you should reduce the volume by another 10-15 per cent.

Control the intensity, pedal cadence and time with a heart-rate monitor or, even better, a power meter. Speed is not an important consid-eration because it depends upon the terrain you are training on, your abilities and on environmental conditions; therefore the training programmes are based on time instead of distance. Never be a slave to your training programme. If you are injured or sick for several days, especially if you have fever, don't try to hang on to your programme. You should allow your body to recover and once you are fit again you should gradually build back up over a period of a few or even several weeks.

Remember, your success in compe-tition will come from the right mix of training and recovery, not by increasing your distances day after day. And don't forget to eat often on your long rides. You should always carry enough food and drink with you – ignoring this could result in you seeing stars and suffering a feeling of complete emptiness. These are typical symptoms of 'bonking' and should be avoided at all costs.

Remember, always check with your physician before starting a training programme if you have any doubts about your health.

The importance of tapering

Tapering aims to eliminate training induced fatigue while maintaining – or even upgrading – training-associated adaptations. It is the final segment of a training period preceding an important competitive event in your season and helps you to avoid overtraining. Its purpose is the recovery of freshness, reducing the physiological and psycho-logical stress of daily training and optimizing race performance.

Pioneering studies with swimmers by sports scientist Dave Costill showed that when they reduced their usual training load from a massive 10,000 yards (9,144 metres) per day to a more modest 3,200 yards (2,926 metres) per day over a 15-day period, their times improved by almost four per cent while their arm strength rose nearly 25 per cent.

Although there is little doubt that tapering is beneficial, there continues to be a debate about how to successfully plan and implement tapering techniques. Some athletes think of a tapering period as a time for easy training and they don't change their volume or frequency of training very much but do cut out most of the intense work.

Every athlete in the sport has his or her own physical and emotional requirements so implementing correct tapering techniques remains an individual issue. There are, however, certain factors that are useful for everyone and these are outlined below.

- The primary aim of tapering is to reduce physiological fatigue from preliminary training for important competitions.
- For cyclists, tapering periods vary in length from a minimum of four days to maximum of 10 days, depending on the individual and the type of event.
- Continue to ride. Don't simply lie on the couch resting. Training volume should be reduced progressively so you end up riding from 30 per cent to 40 per cent of your usual riding distance.
- It's a good idea to keep up certain intensity levels, however, allowing your body to keep in the balance it reached during training. You should maintain your average rhythm and intensity even as training volume is reduced. The higher intensity guarantees that you retain the muscle enzymes that help you process lactate. The fast riding also means that your neuromuscular system will be accustomed to going fast when you ask it to during the event.
- Weekly training frequency should be maintained, according to your training habits and performance level, even though in certain cases it's helpful to insert one or more supplemental days of complete rest. This type of taper works because it combines rest with intensity. It allows recovery but still encourages speed.

Building your training programme

Progressive development

1. Progression is a key requirement. Sessions must be planned in a way that you allow your body to adapt to gradual increases in intensity and volume of your training programme.
2. The training programme should be designed to reach a peak just in time for your goal event.
3. After two weeks of increasing training volume and intensity you should allow your body to adapt to the training impulses in the third week. A recovery week enables you to regain energy and strength and to prepare mentally and physically for the next 'load block'. It also helps to prevent over-training. This happens when you've ridden a lot without adequate recovery – and just when you feel your hard work should be making you better, you find yourself getting worse.

Systematic structure

1. Stability in your training programme is another key requirement. To have an improvement you have to ride at least three-four times per week during a prolonged period.

2. The intensity of your sessions must be controlled using a heart-rate and pedal-cadence monitor. Power measuring devices allow you to control your intensity better.
3. Specificity of your training programme is necessary to tailor it to your needs. The specificity principle says that if you want to become good at something you need to do that thing. So, if for example, if you want to outclass your friends in time trialling, then there is no need to continuously increase the distance of your bicycle rides.
4. Recovery between your sessions is of paramount importance to improve your condition.

Periodization

The training year (macrocycle) is divided into five periods of time (mesocycles) with different goals and activities for each period, which are then further divided into weekly training cycles (microcycles). Within each period you try to control the training volume, intensity, frequency and skill work to direct yourself toward a peak performance. The mesocycles are:

1. *Foundation phase*. Training is mostly based on low intensity, aerobic sessions; you will spend most of the time in Level 1 (See Training intensity levels on

pages 146-149). The workout volume gradually increases but remains relatively low to help you deal with resistance training on the bicycle and with free weights/machines. You should spend three days per week in the gymnasium. Cross training can be integrated as an additional element to maintain a high level of aerobic conditioning and to work on upper body and torso power. This period generally lasts for the first six weeks of the training cycle.

2. *Preparation phase*. In this period you significantly increase your workout volume. Intensity shifts more towards Level 2 with some Level 3 (See Training intensity levels on pages 146-149) as well. You skip the cross training and reduce the number of days with resistance training in the gymnasium from three to two. This period is the next six weeks of the training cycle.

3. *Specialization phase*. This is the last phase before you reach your best condition. At this point, racing starts to enter your programme. Training must be specific to the needs of competition and is no longer focused only on developing the aerobic energy system. Training sessions behind a motorcycle or scooter to support race-specific high-speed coordination become increasingly important. There should be two days per week of resistance training in the gym. This continues for one month.

4. *Competition phase*. You should have a perfect basic condition when you enter this phase. The competition period with the most important races of the season varies in length but for an amateur elite cyclist it can last for a number of months. You cannot maintain a top performance level for such a long period. For

this reason you should schedule several recovery phases after reaching your peak form. Afterwards you start to build up again and 'fine tune' your condition. You should work on strength training with free weights and machines for a minimum of one day per week to maintain the benefits of your winter training programme in the gymnasium.

5. *Transition phase*. This period starts as soon as you have finished the last race of your season and it should last for about a month. After a season of hard training and racing, you really need a period to recover emotionally and physically from the bicycle. Although you should dramatically decrease your daily distances and intensities, you should stay in touch with the road. Don't get off your bicycle completely!

Training intensity levels

Endurance

If you want to be a successful road cyclist you will have to build-up the weekly distances of your stamina training. You achieve this build-up of stamina by increasing your aerobic fitness. Endurance training is the basic training that improves your aerobic energy system and allows you to feel at ease on the bicycle for extended periods without exhausting all your energy.

If you only do endurance training though you will not possess the explosive power and speed to be successful in time trialing, chasing down breakaways, attacking short, steep hills, or sprinting in the race to the finish line.

All kind of factors like the time of the season, your goals, abilities, schedule, weather, environmental conditions, and so on, affect the total number of kilometres you will be able to spend on the saddle. As a general rule, the longest of these sessions should not exceed more than 110 per cent of the distance at which you are planning to compete.

Don't feel tempted to ride too fast; to produce the desired effects you should maintain a pulse rate of 60-80 per cent of your maximum heart rate, or 40-90 per cent of power at your anaerobic threshold.

Control your intensity with a heart-rate monitor and/or power-measuring device.

Level 1, Slow (S)

This level is at slow pace/speed and is the basis of every training programme. It enhances your overall resistance and you get used to staying on your bicycle for a long time. You have to spend most of your training time in this intensity zone. It is crucial for active recovery after high-intensity sessions as well.

The duration of rides at this intensity vary from at least one hour to five hours for an amateur. Professional cyclists sometimes ride at this intensity for up to seven hours. The intensity of this type of training is at 65-80 per cent of your maximum heart rate or 40-70 per cent of power at your anaerobic threshold.

A long Level 1 ride should be undertaken at least once per week with the aim to promote the following in your body's system:
1. To improve your body's ability to metabolize fat as a source of energy. This is especially beneficial for long races.
2. To improve your body's circulatory system (providing the force to keep the blood flowing along the arteries and veins and thus carrying oxygen from the lungs to the tissues, removing waste products from the tissues to lungs and kidneys, bringing new blood and hence oxygen/fuel to your body's cells).
3. Furthermore, this low-intensity level brings about increased neuromuscular efficiency and therefore is ideal for improving basic skills, adjusting riding technique and acclimatizing your body to long periods in the saddle. During Level 1 training, high pedal cadences of 90-100 RPM on flat roads are used to promote a fluent and efficient pedalling style.

Level 2, Medium (M)

This level is at medium pace/speed and is the training intensity at which the major biological mechanisms that determine your performance as a cyclist start to become taxed. It is a more challenging effort for your body than Level 1. This level will enhance your endurance, specifically your capability to optimize your energetic metabolism under effort.

Without a proper Level 2 training load (volume), lasting improvements are not possible. The majority of the specific high spinning and uphill sessions are performed within Level 2 range. Training at Level 2 intensity consists of rides

of between one and two hours, at 80 to 90 per cent of your maximum heart rate or 70-90 per cent of power at the anaerobic threshold. Breathing rate becomes more rhythmic and is noticeably deeper. Conversation is possible, but frequent pauses are necessary to regain breathing pattern. The aim is to:

1. Improve your body's respiratory system, bringing more oxygen to your circulatory system.
2. Enhance your body's ability to use fat as a fuel source in preference to the all-important carbohydrate stores.
3. Force your body to continuously recruit, within the working muscles, as many muscle fibres as possible in order to obtain adequate supplies of muscle glycogen.

Tempo training
Tempo training is Level 3 intensity. Provided you have the proper aerobic foundation, built properly from endurance work, this could be the level of training your cycling has been lacking.

Level 3, Tempo (T)
This level is at high pace/speed. It is a step up from Level 2 intensity. Level 3 is close to, and fluctuates with, the anaerobic threshold value at 90-95 per cent of your maximum

heart rate or 90-100 per cent of power at your anaerobic threshold. The purpose of this level is to gradually increase your anaerobic threshold, avoiding excessive lactic acid amounts. Sessions at this level may normally only be sustained for up to 40 minutes.

This training can be done both with short intervals of 20-180 second-long intervals from three to 20 minutes (aerobic interval training). It can be very effectively executed on an ergometer, especially during cold winter days and when you are not able to train in a mountainous environment. Level 3 training requires intense concentration and is psychologically very demanding.

- Level 3 training places a very high load on your body's ability to supply oxygen to the working muscles.
- Equally important, it stresses the mechanisms that control the fatigue-causing processes that occur within the muscles at high work rates.
- Level 3 training will accustom your body to the physical load that will be encountered in most racing situations.

Interval training
Level 4, Maximum (MX)
This level is at a very high pace/speed. Level 4 training is based

on repetitions of intervals of hard effort and recovery, with the work efforts near, or at your maximum heart rate. Training at Level 4 requires you to work at intervals of intensity above your critical threshold, so steady-state exercise is no longer physically possible.

The aim of this type of training is to improve your body's ability to work at levels of intensity where oxygen cannot be delivered to muscle cells fast enough. The cells will use fuel stored within them, rather than oxygen delivered in the blood stream. This causes lactic acid to build up and begins to break down (fatigue) muscle fibres. Level 4 is the most demanding form of training both physically and psychologically but it cannot replace the vital endurance training as performed at Levels 2 and 3.

Training programmes

Training programme for week 1 (First week of Foundation phase)

Day	Training description	Intensity level	Hours	Strength training
Mon	Recovery of agility after strength training; pedal cadence 95-110 RPM	1	1	Yes
Tue	Endurance training with 2x5-10 min M; pedal cadence uphill 80-90 RPM, on flat roads 90-100 RPM	1-2	2	
Wed	Recovery of agility after strength training; pedal cadence 100-110 RPM	1	1	Yes
Thu	Rest			
Fri	Recovery of agility after strength training; pedal cadence 90-100 RPM	1	1	Yes
Sat	Endurance training with 3x7 min M. Focus on maintaining a high pedal cadence of 80-90 RPM uphill and/or 100 RPM on flat roads	1-2	3	
Sun	Endurance training off the road bicycle (mountain bicycle, hiking, running, cross-country skiing)	1-2	2-2.5	

Training programme for week 2 (Second week of Foundation phase)

Day	Training description	Intensity level	Hours	Strength training
Mon	Recovery of agility after strength training; pedal cadence 95-100 RPM	1	1	Yes
Tue	Endurance training with 5 downhill sprints of 20 sec and 2x10 min M; pedal cadence uphill 60-70 RPM, on flat roads 95-100 RPM	1-2	2.5	
Wed	Recovery of agility after strength training; pedal cadence 90-100 RPM	1	1	Yes
Thu	Rest			
Fri	Recovery of agility after strength training; pedal cadence 90-100 RPM	1	1	Yes
Sat	Endurance training with 3x10 min M. Focus on maintaining a high pedal cadence of 80-90 RPM uphill and/or 100 RPM on flat roads	1-2	3.5	
Sun	Endurance training off the road bicycle (mountain bicycle, hiking, running, cross-country skiing) with one short effort of 1-3 minutes T	1-3	3	

Training programme for week 3 (Third week of Foundation phase)

Day	Training description	Intensity level	Hours	Strength training
Mon	Recovery of agility after strength training; pedal cadence 95-110 RPM	1	1	Yes
Tue	Easy endurance training; pedal cadence 85-100 RPM	1	1.5	
Wed	Recovery of agility after strength training; pedal cadence 100-110 RPM	1	0.5	Yes
Thu	Rest		1	
Fri	Recovery of agility after strength training; pedal cadence 90-100 RPM	1	2.5	Yes
Sat	Endurance training with 3x5 min M. Focus on maintaining a high pedal cadence of 80-90 RPM uphill and/or 100 RPM on flat roads	1-2	2	
Sun	Endurance training off the road bicycle (mountain bicycle, hiking, running, cross-country skiing)	1-2	3	

Training programme for week 4 (Fourth week of Foundation phase)

Day	Training description	Intensity level	Hours	Strength training
Mon	Recovery of agility after strength training; pedal cadence 95-100 RPM	1	1	Yes
Tue	Endurance training with 5 downhill sprints of 20 sec and 3x10 min M; pedal cadence uphill 60-70 RPM, on flat roads 95-100 RPM	1-2	3	
Wed	Recovery of agility after strength training; pedal cadence 90-100 RPM	1	2	Yes
Thu	Rest			
Fri	Recovery of agility after strength training; pedal cadence 100-110 RPM	1	2	Yes
Sat	Endurance training with 5 downhill sprints of 20 sec and 3x12 min M – 1 min T. Focus on maintaining a high pedal cadence of 80-90 RPM uphill and/or 100 RPM on flat roads	1-2-3	3.5	
Sun	Endurance training off the road bicycle (mountain bicycle, hiking, running, cross-country skiing) with a few short efforts of 1-3 minutes T	1-2-3	3.5	

Training programme for week 5 (Fifth week of Foundation phase)

Day	Training description	Intensity level	Hours	Strength training
Mon	Recovery of agility after strength training; pedal cadence 95-110 RPM	1	2	Yes
Tue	Endurance training with 6 downhill sprints of 20 sec and 4x10 min M; pedal cadence uphill 60-70 RPM, on flat roads 95-100 RPM	1-2	3.5	
Wed	Recovery of agility after strength training; pedal cadence 90-100 RPM	1	1	Yes
Thu	Rest			
Fri	Recovery of agility after strength training; pedal cadence 100-115 RPM	1	2	Yes
Sat	Endurance training with 6 downhill sprints of 20 sec and 3x15 min M – 1 min T. Focus on maintaining a high pedal cadence of 80-90 RPM uphill and/or 100 RPM on flat roads	1-2-3	4	
Sun	Endurance training off the road bicycle (mountain bicycle, hiking, running, cross-country skiing) with a few short efforts of 1-3 minutes T	1-2-3	4	

Training programme for week 6 (Sixth week of Foundation phase)

Day	Training description	Intensity level	Hours	Strength training
Mon	Recovery of agility after strength training; pedal cadence 95-110 RPM	1	1	Yes
Tue	Easy endurance training; pedal cadence 85-100 RPM	1	2	
Wed	Recovery of agility after strength training; pedal cadence 100-110 RPM	1	0.5	Yes
Thu	Rest			
Fri	Recovery of agility after strength training; pedal cadence 90-100 RPM	1	1	Yes
Sat	Endurance training with 3x5 min M. Focus on maintaining a high pedal cadence of 80-90 RPM uphill and/or 100 RPM on flat roads	1-2	2.5	
Sun	Endurance training off the road bicycle (mountain bicycle, hiking, running, cross-country skiing)	1-2	2.5	

Training programme for week 7 (First week of Preparation phase)

Day	Training description	Intensity level	Hours	Strength training
Mon	Recovery of agility after strength training; pedal cadence 95-110 RPM	1	1.5	Yes
Tue	Aerobic strength interval training with 2 series of 10x20 sec T – 40 sec S-M uphill. Pedal cadence while T from 40 RPM to 70 RPM and while S-M around 50-70 RPM. 10 min S between series. Power levels while T should increase till 200 per cent of anaerobic threshold power. But heart rate shouldn't exceed AT! Afterwards 2 series of 3x15 sec sprints at maximum speed on a flat road with 52–53x14. 5 min active recovery (S) between sprints and 10 min between series. Jump when you are riding 20 kph (12 mph)	1-2-3-4	3	
Wed	Endurance training with 3x15 min M – 3 min T. Alternate 5 min with a pedal cadence of 60 RPM and 5 min with 90 RPM. 2 series uphill, 1 series on flat roads (3 min T with 90 RPM)	1-2-3	3.5	
Thu	Rest			
Fri	Recovery of agility after strength training; pedal cadence 100-115 RPM	1	1.5	Yes
Sat	Aerobic strength interval training with 2 series of 10x20 sec T – 40 sec S-M uphill. Pedal cadence while T from 40 RPM to 70 RPM and while S-M around 50-70 RPM. 10 min S between series. Power levels while T should increase till 200 per cent of anaerobic threshold power. But heart rate shouldn't exceed AT! Afterwards 2 series of 3x15 sec sprints at maximum speed on a flat road with 52–53x14. 5 min active recovery (lento) between sprints and 10 min between series. Jump when you are riding 20 kph (12 mph)	1-2-3-4	3.5	
Sun	Endurance training with 6 downhill sprints of 20 sec and 3x15 min M – 3 min T. Focus on maintaining a high pedal cadence of 80-90 RPM uphill and/or 100 RPM on flat roads	1-2-3	4	

Training programme for week 8 (Second week of Preparation phase)

Day	Training description	Intensity level	Hours	Strength training
Mon	Recovery of agility after strength training; pedal cadence 95-110 RPM	1	1.5	Yes
Tue	Aerobic strength interval training with 3 series of 10x20 sec T – 40 sec S-M uphill. Pedal cadence while T from 40 RPM to 70 RPM and while S-M around 50-70 RPM. 10 min S between series. Power levels while T should increase till 200 per cent of anaerobic threshold power. But heart rate shouldn't exceed AT! Afterwards 2 series of 3x20 sec sprints at maximum speed on a flat road with 52–53x14. 5 min active recovery (S) between sprints and 10 min between series. Jump when you are riding 20 kph (12 mph)	1-2-3-4	3	
Wed	Endurance training with 3x20 min M – 3 min T. Alternate 5 min with a pedal cadence of 60 RPM and 5 min with 90 RPM. 2 series uphill, 1 series on flat roads (3 min T with 90 RPM)	1-2-3	4	
Thu	Rest			
Fri	Recovery of agility after strength training; pedal cadence 100-115 RPM	1	1.5	Yes
Sat	Aerobic strength interval training with 3 series of 10x20 sec T – 40 sec S-M uphill. Pedal cadence while T from 40 RPM to 70 RPM and while S-M around 50-70 RPM. 10 min L between series. Power levels while T should increase till 200 per cent of anaerobic threshold power. But heart rate shouldn't exceed AT! Afterwards 2 series of 3x20 sec sprints at maximum speed on a flat road with 52–53x14. 5 min active recovery (S) between sprints and 10 min between series. Jump when you are riding 20 kph (12 mph)	1-2-3-4	3.5	
Sun	Endurance training with 6 downhill sprints of 20 sec and 3x15 min M – 3 min T. Focus on maintaining a high pedal cadence of 80-90 RPM uphill and/or 100 RPM on flat roads	1-2-3	4.5	

Training programme for week 9 (Third week of Preparation phase)

Day	Training description	Intensity level	Hours	Strength training
Mon	Easy endurance training; pedal cadence 80-90 RPM	1	1.5	Yes
Tue	Lactate threshold test in laboratory or field test	1-2-3-4	1	
Wed	Endurance training with 3x10 min M. Focus on maintaining a high pedal cadence of 80-90 RPM uphill and/or 100 RPM on flat roads	1-2-3	2.5	
Thu	Rest			
Fri	Recovery of agility after strength training; pedal cadence 100-115 RPM	1	1	Yes
Sat	Aerobic strength interval training with 3 series of 5x20 sec T – 40 sec S-M uphill. Pedal cadence while T from 40 RPM to 70 RPM and while S-M around 50-70 RPM. 10 min S between series. Power levels while T should increase till 200 per cent of anaerobic threshold power. But heart rate shouldn't exceed AT! Afterwards 2 series of 3x15 sec sprints at maximum speed on a flat road with 52–53x14. 5 min active recovery (S) between sprints and 10 min between series. Jump when you are riding 20 kph (12 mph)	1-2-3-4	2	
Sun	Endurance training with 3x10 min M – 1 min T. Focus on maintaining a high pedal cadence of 80-90 RPM uphill and/or 100 RPM on flat roads	1-2-3	2.5	

Training programme for week 10 (Fourth week of Preparation phase)

Day	Training description	Intensity level	Hours	Strength training
Mon	Recovery of agility after strength training; pedal cadence 95-110 RPM	1	1.5	Yes
Tue	Aerobic strength interval training with 4 series of 10x20 sec T – 40 sec S-M uphill. Pedal cadence while T from 40 RPM to 70 RPM and while S-M around 50-70 RPM. 10 min S between series. Power levels while T should increase till 200 per cent of anaerobic threshold power. But heart rate shouldn't exceed AT! Afterwards 2 series of 4x20 sec sprints at maximum speed on a flat road with 52–53x14. 5 min active recovery (S) between sprints and 10 min between series. Jump when you are riding 20 kph (12 mph)	1-2-3-4	3.5	
Wed	Endurance training with 3x25 min M – 5 min T. Alternate 5 min with a pedal cadence of 60 RPM and 5 min with 90 RPM. 2 series uphill, 1 series on flat roads	1-2-3	4	
Thu	Rest			
Fri	Recovery of agility after strength training; pedal cadence 100-115 RPM	1	1.5	Yes
Sat	Aerobic strength interval training with 4 series of 10x20 sec T – 40 sec S-M uphill. Pedal cadence while T from 40 RPM to 70 RPM and while S-M around 50-70 RPM. 10 min S between series. Power levels while T should increase till 200 per cent of anaerobic threshold power. But heart rate shouldn't exceed AT! Afterwards 2 series of 4x20 sec sprints at maximum speed on a flat road with 52–53x14. 5 min active recovery (S) between sprints and 10 min between series. Jump when you are riding 20 kph (12 mph)	1-2-3-4	4	
Sun	Endurance training with 6 downhill sprints of 20 sec and 3x20 min M – 3 min T. Focus on maintaining a high pedal cadence of 80-90 RPM uphill and/or 100 RPM on flat roads	1-2-3	4.5	

Training programme for week 11 (Fifth week of Preparation phase)

Day	Training description	Intensity level	Hours	Strength training
Mon	Recovery of agility after strength training; pedal cadence 95-110 RPM	1	1.5	Yes
Tue	Aerobic strength interval training with 4 series of 10x20 sec T – 40 sec S-M uphill. Pedal cadence while T from 40 RPM to 70 RPM and while S-M around 50-70 RPM. 10 min S between series. Power levels while T should increase till 200 per cent of anaerobic threshold power. But heart rate shouldn't exceed AT! Afterwards 2 series of 4x20 sec sprints at maximum speed on a flat road with 52–53x13. 5 min active recovery (S) between sprints and 10 min between series. Jump when you are riding 20 kph (12 mph)	1-2-3-4	4	
Wed	Endurance training with 3x30 min M – 5 min T. Alternate 5 min with a pedal cadence of 60 RPM and 5 min with 90 RPM. 2 series uphill, 1 series on flat roads	1-2-3	4.5	
Thu	Rest			
Fri	Recovery of agility after strength training; pedal cadence 100-115 RPM	1	1.5	Yes
Sat	Aerobic strength interval training with 4 series of 10x20 sec T – 40 sec S-M uphill. Pedal cadence while T from 40 RPM to 70 RPM and while S-M around 50-70 RPM. 10 min S between series. Power levels while T should increase till 200 per cent of anaerobic threshold power. But heart rate shouldn't exceed AT! Afterwards 2 series of 3x20 sec sprints at maximum speed on a flat road with 52–53x13. 5 min active recovery (S) between sprints and 10 min between series. Jump when you are riding 20 kph (12 mph)	1-2-3-4	4	
Sun	Endurance training with 6 downhill sprints of 20 sec and 3x25 min M – 3 min T. Focus on maintaining a high pedal cadence of 80-90 RPM uphill and/or 100 RPM on flat roads	1-2-3	5	

Training programme for week 12 (Sixth week of Preparation phase)

Day	Training description	Intensity level	Hours	Strength training
Mon	Recovery of agility after strength training; pedal cadence 90-100 RPM	1	1	Yes
Tue	Aerobic strength interval training with 2 series of 10x20 sec T – 40 sec S-M uphill. Pedal cadence while T from 40 RPM to 70 RPM and while S-M around 50-70 RPM. 10 min S between series. Power levels while T should increase till 200 per cent of anaerobic threshold power. But heart rate shouldn't exceed AT! Afterwards 1 series of 3x20 sec sprints at maximum speed on a flat road with 52–53x13. 1 min 40 sec active recovery (S) between sprints and 10 min between series. Jump when you are riding 20 kph (12 mph)	1-2-3-4	2	
Wed	Endurance training with 3x10 min M. Focus on maintaining a high pedal cadence of 80-90 RPM uphill and/or 100 RPM on flat roads	1-2-3	2.5	
Thu	Rest			
Fri	Recovery of agility after strength training; pedal cadence 100-115 RPM	1	1	Yes
Sat	Aerobic strength interval training with 2 series of 10x20 sec T – 40 sec S-M uphill. Pedal cadence while T from 40 RPM to 70 RPM and while S-M around 50-70 RPM. 10 min S between series. Power levels while T should increase till 200 per cent of anaerobic threshold power. But heart rate shouldn't exceed AT! Afterwards 1 series of 3x20 sec sprints at maximum speed on a flat road with 52–53x13. 1 min 40 sec active recovery (S) between sprints and 10 min between series. Jump when you are riding 20 kph (12 mph)	1-2-3-4	2	
Sun	Endurance training with 3x10 min M – 1 min T. Focus on maintaining a high pedal cadence of 80-90 RPM uphill and/or 100 RPM on flat roads	1-2-3	2.5	

Training programme for week 13 (First week of Specialization phase)

Day	Training description	Intensity level	Hours	Strength training
Mon	Hill sprint training after the strength training in the gym; 2 series of 5x12 sec. Start the exercise when you ride very slowly and jump, almost from a standstill, in an all-out sprint while staying seated the whole way to the top. After each uphill sprint recover 2 minutes using a light gear to release the muscle tension. Between series 10 min S	1-4	2	Yes
Tue	Aerobic strength interval training with 4 series of 4 min T 50 RPM – 4 min T 90 RPM uphill. 10 min S between series. Afterwards interval training; 1 series of 4x20 sec sprints at maximum speed on a flat road with 52–53x13. 1 min 40 sec active recovery (S) between sprints and 10 min between series. Jump when you are riding 20 kph (12 mph)	1-3-4	3	
Wed	Endurance training with 3x30 min M. Focus on maintaining a high pedal cadence of 80-90 RPM uphill and/or 100 RPM on flat roads	1-2	4	
Thu	Rest			
Fri	Hill sprint training after the strength training in the gym; 2 series of 5x12 sec. Start the exercise when you ride very slowly and jump, almost from a standstill, in an all-out sprint while staying seated the whole way to the top. After each uphill sprint recover 2 minutes using a light gear to release the muscle tension. Between series 10 min S	1-4	2	Yes
Sat	Aerobic strength interval training with 4 series of 4 min T 50 RPM – 4 min T 90 RPM uphill. 10 min S between series. Afterwards interval training; 1 series of 4x20 sec sprints at maximum speed on a flat road with 52–53x13. 1 min 40 sec active recovery (S) between sprints and 10 min between series. Jump when you are riding 20 kph (12 mph)	1-3-4	3	
Sun	Endurance training with 3x25 min M – 5 min T. Do 2 series uphill while maintaining a high pedal cadence of 80-90 RPM uphill. In the second part of the training ride do 1 series of 25 min M and 5 min T behind a scooter or motorcycle while maintaining a pedal cadence of 105-110 RPM	1-2-3	4.5	

Training programme for week 14 (Second week of Specialization phase)

Day	Training description	Intensity level	Hours	Strength training
Mon	Easy endurance training	1	1.5	
Tue	Hill sprint training after the strength training in the gym; 2 series of 6x12 sec. Start the exercise when you ride very slowly and jump, almost from a standstill, in an all-out sprint while staying seated the whole way to the top. After each uphill sprint recover 2 minutes using a light gear to release the muscle tension. Between series 10 min S	1-4	2	Yes
Wed	Endurance training with 3x20 min M – 10 min T. Alternate 5 min with a pedal cadence of 60 RPM and 5 min with 90 RPM. 2 series uphill, 1 series on flat roads	1-2-3	4.5	
Thu	Rest			
Fri	Hill sprint training after the strength training in the gym; 2 series of 6x12 sec. Start the exercise when you ride very slowly and jump, almost from a standstill, in an all-out sprint while staying seated the whole way to the top. After each uphill sprint recover 2 minutes using a light gear to release the muscle tension. Between series 10 min S	1-4	2	Yes
Sat	Aerobic strength interval training with 5 series of 4 min T 50 RPM – 4 min T 90 RPM uphill. 10 min S between series. Afterwards interval training; 2 series of 3x20 sec sprints out of the saddle at maximum speed on a flat road with 52–53x13. 1 min 40 sec active recovery (S) between sprints and 10 min between series. Jump when you are riding 20 kph (12 mph)	1-3-4	4	
Sun	Endurance training with 3x(25 min M – 10 min T – 1 min MX). Do 2 series uphill while maintaining a high pedal cadence of 80-90 RPM uphill. In the second part of the training ride do 1 series of 25 min M, 10 min T and finalize with 1 minute flat out (MX) behind a scooter or motorcycle while maintaining a pedal cadence of 105-110 RPM	1-2-3-4	5	

Training programme for week 15 (Third week of Specialization phase)

Day	Training description	Intensity level	Hours	Strength training
Mon	Easy endurance training	1	1.5	
Tue	Hill sprint training after the strength training in the gym; 2 series of 8x12 sec. Start the exercise when you ride very slowly and jump with a big gear, almost from a standstill, in an all-out sprint while staying seated the whole way to the top. After each uphill sprint recover 2 minutes using a light gear to release the muscle tension. Between series 10 min S	1-4	3	Yes
Wed	Endurance training with 3x20 min M – 15 min T – 1 min MX. Alternate 5 min with a pedal cadence of 70 RPM and 5 min with 100 RPM. 2 series uphill, 1 series on flat roads	1-2-3-4	4.5	
Thu	Rest			
Fri	Hill sprint training after the strength training in the gym; 2 series of 8x12 sec. Start the exercise when you ride very slowly and jump with a big gear, almost from a standstill, in an all-out sprint while staying seated the whole way to the top. After each uphill sprint recover 2 minutes using a light gear to release the muscle tension. Between series 10 min S	1-4	3	Yes
Sat	Aerobic strength interval training with 5 series of 4 min T 50 RPM – 4 min T 90 RPM uphill. 10 min S between series. Afterwards interval training; 2 series of 3x20 sec sprints out of the saddle at maximum speed on a flat road with 52–53x13. 1 min 40 sec active recovery (S) between sprints and 10 min between series. Jump when you are riding 20 kph (12 mph)	1-3-4	4	
Sun	Endurance training with 3x(25 min M – 10 min T – 2 min MX). Do 2 series uphill while maintaining a high pedal cadence of 80-90 RPM uphill. In the second part of ride do 1 series of 25 min M, 10 min T and finish with 1 min MX behind a scooter or motorcycle of 15 min M, 5 min T and finalize with a sprint of 20 sec (MX) while maintaining a pedal cadence of 105-110 RPM	1-2-3-4	5	

Training programme for week 16 (Fourth week of Specialization phase)

Day	Training description	Intensity level	Hours	Strength training
Mon	Easy endurance training	1	1	
Tue	Hill sprint training after the strength training in the gym; 2 series of 4x10 sec. Start the exercise when you ride very slowly and jump with a big gear, almost from a standstill, in an all-out sprint while staying seated the whole way to the top. After each uphill sprint recover 2 minutes using a light gear to release the muscle tension. Between series 10 min S	1-4	1.5	Yes
Wed	Endurance training with 3x10 min M – 5 min T. Alternate 5 min with a pedal cadence of 70 RPM and 5 min with 100 RPM. 2 series uphill, 1 series on flat roads	1-2-3	2.5	
Thu	Rest			
Fri	Hill sprint training after the strength training in the gym; 2 series of 4x10 sec. Start the exercise when you ride very slowly and jump with a big gear, almost from a standstill, in an all-out sprint while staying seated the whole way to the top. After each uphill sprint recover 2 minutes using a light gear to release the muscle tension. Between series 10 min S	1-4	1.5	Yes
Sat	Aerobic strength interval training with 3 series of 3 min T 50 RPM – 3 min T 90 RPM uphill. 10 min S between series. Afterwards interval training; 1 series of 3x20 sec sprints out of the saddle at maximum speed on a flat road with 52–53x13. 1 min 40 sec active recovery (S) between sprints and 10 min between series. Jump when you are riding 20 kph (12 mph)	1-3-4	2	
Sun	Endurance training with 3x12 min M – 5 min T. Do 2 series uphill while maintaining a high pedal cadence of 80-90 RPM uphill. In the second part of the training ride do 1 series behind a scooter or motorcycle of 15 min M, 5 min T and finalize with a sprint of 20 sec (MX) while maintaining a pedal cadence of 105-110 RPM	1-2-3-4	2.5	

Training programme for week 17 (First week of Competition phase)

Day	Training description	Intensity level	Hours	Strength training
Mon	Easy endurance training; recovery of agility after strength training	1	1	Yes
Tue	Aerobic interval training with 3 series of 10x40 sec T – 20 sec S uphill. Pedal cadence while T should increase from 60 RPM to 90 RPM and while S around 60-70 RPM. 10 min S between series. Power levels while T should increase till 110 per cent of anaerobic threshold power. But heart rate shouldn't exceed AT!	1-3	3.5	
Wed	Endurance training with 3x25 min M – 5 min T. Alternate 5 min with a pedal cadence of 60 RPM and 5 min with 100 RPM. 2 series uphill, 1 series on flat roads	1-2-3	5	
Thu	Rest			
Fri	Easy endurance training with 3 ins and outs of 20 sec to improve speed. Recovery (S) between sprints minimum 5 min!	1-4	2	
Sat	Easy endurance training	1	1	
Sun	150 km road race	1-2-3-4	4	

Training programme for week 18 (Second week of Competition phase)

Day	Training description	Intensity level	Hours	Strength training
Mon	Do a strength training at 50 per cent (sets and repetitions reduced by 50 per cent of normal values)	1	1	Yes (50%)
Tue	Endurance riding for 3 to 4 hours on mixed terrain at slow and medium intensity	1-2	3.5	
Wed	Rest			
Thu	Easy endurance training	1	1	
Fri	First stage of a stage race (prologue). Warm up at least 30 min!	1-2-3-4	1	
Sat	Second stage	1-2-3-4	4	
Sun	Third stage	1-2-3-4	4	

Training programme for week 19 (Third week of Competition phase)

Day	Training description	Intensity level	Hours	Strength training
Mon	Easy endurance training	1	1.5	
Tue	Recovery of agility after strength training	1	1	Yes
Wed	Aerobic interval training with 3 series of 10x40 sec T – 20 sec S uphill. Pedal cadence while T should increase from 60 RPM to 90 RPM and while S around 60-70 RPM. 10 min S between series. Power levels while T should increase till 110 per cent of anaerobic threshold power. But heart rate shouldn't exceed AT!	1-3	3.5	
Thu	Endurance training with 3x25 min M . Alternate 5 min with a pedal cadence of 60 RPM and 5 min with 90 RPM. 2 series uphill, 1 series on flat roads	1-2	4-4.5	
Fri	Rest			
Sat	Easy endurance training	1	1	
Sun	Road race 160 km	1-2-3-4	4	

Training programme for week 20 (Fourth week of Competition phase)

Day	Training description	Intensity level	Hours	Strength training
Mon	Endurance training	1-2	5	
Tue	Rest	1	1	
Wed	Do a strength training at 50 per cent (sets and repetitions reduced by 50 per cent of normal values). Afterwards hill strength training; 2 series of 5x12 sec. Start the exercise when you ride very slowly and jump, almost from a standstill, in an all-out sprint while staying seated the whole way to the top. After each uphill sprint recover 2 minutes using a light gear to release the muscle tension. Between series 10 min S	1-4	2	Yes (50%)
Thu	Endurance training with 3x20 min M . Alternate 5 min with a pedal cadence of 60 RPM and 5 min with 90 RPM. 2 series uphill, 1 series on flat roads	1-2	4-4.5	
Fri	Rest			
Sat	Easy endurance training	1	1	
Sun	Road race 160 km	1-2-3-4	4	

First published in 2011 by
New Holland Publishers (UK) Ltd
London • Cape Town • Sydney • Auckland
www.newhollandpublishers.com

Garfield House
86–88 Edgware
Road
London W2 2EA
United Kingdom

80 McKenzie
Street
Cape Town 8001
South Africa

Unit 1, 66
Gibbes Street,
Chatswood
NSW 2067
Australia

218 Lake Road
Northcote
Auckland
New Zealand

A catalogue record for this book is available from the British Library.

ISBN 978 1 84773 780 9

This book has been produced for New Holland Publishers by
Chase My Snail Ltd
London • Cape Town

Project Manager: Daniel Ford
Designer: Darren Exell
Photo Editors: Darren Exell and Daniel Ford
Publisher: Guy Hobbs
Production: Marion Storz
Illustrations: Juliet Percival and James Berrangé
Proof reader: Timothy Shave

2 4 6 8 10 9 7 5 3 1

Reproduction by Pica Digital Pte Ltd, Singapore
Printed and bound in Malaysia by Times Offset (Malaysia) Sdn Bhd